MYTHS AND MYSTERIES

OF
KANSAS

TRUE STORIES
OF THE UNSOLVED AND UNEXPLAINED

DIANA LAMBDIN MEYER

gpp

Guilford, Connecticut

D0907463

Copyright © 2012 by Morris Book Publishing, LLC

Map by Daniel Lloyd © Morris Book Publishing, LLC
Project editor: Meredith Dias
Layout: Justin Marciano

Library of Congress Cataloging-in-Publication Data

Meyer, Diana Lambdin.
  Myths and mysteries of Kansas : true stories of the unsolved and unexplained / Diana Lambdin Meyer.
      p. cm. — (Myths and mysteries series)
  Includes bibliographical references and index.
  ISBN 978-0-7627-6446-4
  1. Kansas—History—Anecdotes. 2. Curiosities and wonders—Kansas—Anecdotes. 3. Legends—Kansas. I. Title.
  F681.6.M49 2012
  978.1—dc23

                                        2011032694

Printed in the United States of America

10 9 8 7 6 5 4 3 2 1

2011~12

CONTENTS

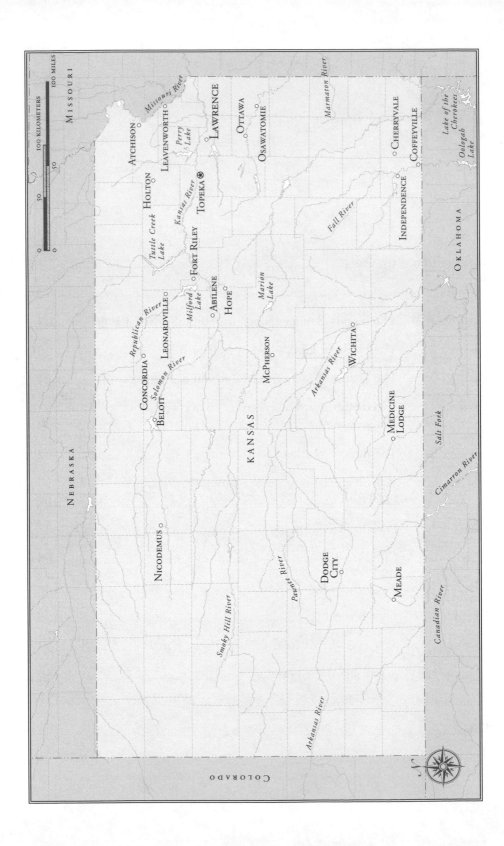

ACKNOWLEDGMENTS

Suddenly I'm very much in awe of those who stand before a global audience at the Academy Awards, so eloquently remembering to thank everyone whose lives have ever touched theirs. On a much smaller scale, this is my Oscar moment. I sure hope I don't forget anyone.

On an unseasonably warm winter day in western Kansas, Angela Bates introduced me to Nicodemus and challenged me to think "what if." She followed up so graciously and with such detail to my many questions that I am forever a fan of little Nicodemus.

Samantha Kenner and Glenda Purkis in Abilene shared their love of their town with me on Valentine's Day, as did Adrian Potter, who operates Abilene's Victorian Inn, the very home where Dwight Eisenhower's influential friend Swede Hazlett once lived. To John Eisenhower, the only surviving son of the late president, who personally took time to respond to my inquiries and share memories of his family, I am most grateful and honored.

A number of people at the Kansas State Historical Society, including Lisa Keys, never failed to answer the phone and my questions. Kelvin Crow, the military historian at Fort

Leavenworth, was equally responsive, informative, and encouraging, allowing me access to his extensive library of research material.

The staff at the Parkville branch of the Mid-Continent Public Library deserves a special thank-you for their numerous searches, special orders, and patience with my impatience.

Of course, no one knows of my impatience more than my husband, Bruce, and our son, Bradley. As always, Bruce shared with me the road and the passion for the subject, while taking great images, spending hours searching through microfiche, and proofreading each chapter. Equal credit goes to Bradley, who feigned interest in my babblings and took care of the kittens while I was away.

And finally, I couldn't have done it without the members of the KAQ, who cheered, encouraged, applauded, and kicked my hindquarters on a daily basis until each and every word in this book was the very best it could be.

INTRODUCTION

I wasn't born in Kansas, nor was I raised here. But the history of Kansas runs through my veins as surely as the DNA I share with my great-great-grandfather Wilford Lambdin, who migrated to Independence, Kansas, in the 1880s. He is buried there, along with my great-great-aunt Amanda. Her life, which ended so violently in 1954, is one of the many mysteries and myths of Kansas. She is certainly a legend in our family.

The legends of Kansas run through all of our veins, whether we first recognize it or not. Kansas is a part of all of us who have ever dreamed of something better; who have ever stood up for what is right; who have fought for and believe in freedom; who have ever pushed the envelope; and who fear a knock at the door in the middle of the night.

The people highlighted in these chapters reflect the best and worst of Kansas and in American history. In reality, they are the best and worst of humankind, and certainly many were an influential part of global history. There are certainly others who are equally intriguing, mysterious, and legendary, but these are the ones I chose.

My hope is that you will dig deep into your own family roots or into the history of Kansas to see how these people have made a difference in your life. You may find a few mysteries, myths, and legends of your own.

CHAPTER 1

The Bloody Benders:
The First Family of Serial Killers

I s it possible that a family of four living on the Kansas prairie got away with serial murder for more than three years and escaped to another part of the country to continue their killing spree?

What does it say about our society that the names and actions of serial killers are as well known as those of legitimate heroes, true leaders, and kindhearted souls who have relieved suffering rather than be the cause of it?

Ted Bundy. Jeffrey Dahmer. Son of Sam. The Green River Killer. The Grim Sleeper.

Their names are ingrained into our human psyche and fascination for the gruesome and fearsome among us.

For the most part, however, only those who study the actions of serial killers or those who today live in or near Labette County in southeast Kansas know the Bender family name and their deadly acts while living here in the 1870s. Many believe that the Benders could have been the first serial killing family in US history.

There are so many unknowns about the Bender family. In fact, there's significant speculation that the four adults were not even related. And much of what was known with certainty at the time has been so inflated by the human capacity for telling a good tale that sharing it with any claim of accuracy nearly 150 years later is next to impossible.

But the one indisputable fact is that a number of honest, hardworking, and innocent people, including a three-year-old girl, died a horrible and painful death at the hands of these people, who have become known as the Bloody Benders.

No one knows for sure where the Benders were before they came to Kansas, but John Sr. spoke German, except for a few four-letter English words, and was often seen reading a German Bible. Pa Bender, as he is called in most accounts, was a large man maybe in his late fifties when he and his son, also John, arrived in Labette County, in the fall of 1870. John spoke fluent English without any trace of German and was said to be slim and tall.

The two men filed adjacent claims of 160 acres each, which as a result of the Homestead Act of 1862 was the standard of the day. Those seeking the American dream of owning land came from around the world as the US government gave away land in exchange for five years of hard work and improvements to the land.

So Pa Bender and his son John didn't attract any undue attention as they traveled by wagon along the Osage Trail from Fort Scott toward Independence, Kansas. They set to work building a house about one hundred yards from the trail, followed by a well, a

BRUCE N. MEYER PHOTO

Kate Bender and Ma Bender

barn, and all the trappings of a prairie homestead. Ma Bender and daughter Kate arrived after the house was built, which was also common for settlers at the time. They soon had a few chickens, ducks, cows, and pigs and a small patch of corn with which to feed the animals. An apple orchard followed the next spring.

Although Pa and John Bender didn't attract much attention, the opposite was the case when Ma and Kate arrived. Ma spoke with a thick German accent and was said to be short, heavyset, and harsh in her appearance. Some accounts describe her charitably as "not very friendly" and others say she was "downright mean."

Aah, but then there was Kate. Kate made up for any ugliness in Ma's physicality or personality. In modern terms, Kate was hot, smokin', a babe. Perhaps in her early twenties, she had auburn hair and a sparkling personality. Endowed with a great body, Kate had a wardrobe that accented her figure. Reports of the day described her as "voluptuous."

They say that Kate was intelligent and a great conversationalist. Some women reported that she flirted with their husbands, but either way, Kate was the energy of the family and probably the brains as well.

John and Kate often went to church together and Kate, not afraid to ride and explore the prairie on her own, took a job for a short while in the spring of 1871 at the Cherryvale Hotel, about six miles away. She captivated the attention of any single and many a married man in southeast Kansas. Several called on her and escorted her to picnics, dances, and social events typical of a prairie community in the 1870s.

Kate didn't work long at the Cherryvale Hotel because the Benders' small family business began to flourish and her help was needed back at home. From the beginning, they had planned to operate a little inn and grocery store from the front half of their home, offering respite to travelers on the trail. Even before the women arrived, John put up a large sign, visible from the trail, that read GROCRY. When Kate arrived, she turned the sign over and painted in more legible letters, GROCERIES.

It's hard to estimate how many people traveled the Osage Trail, which was located about where Highway 169 is today. It was certainly not a major interstate highway, but this was where a lot of growth took place in the United States during the 1870s. Immigrants were moving to North America in record numbers. Civil War veterans and freed slaves were starting a new life in the unoccupied lands of the West. Missionaries were ministering to the American Indians who had been removed to Oklahoma, just about fifteen miles south of where the Bender family had settled.

In May 1871 a man's body was discovered in a nearby creek, his skull smashed and his throat slashed from ear to ear. No one knew who he was, and though they were concerned about the violent nature of his death, risk was a part of the lifestyle on the prairie at this time. He was buried in the church cemetery and everyone went on with their lives.

In the coming months, word came through the larger communities of Fort Scott and Independence that folks back east were concerned for the whereabouts of missing relatives, menfolk who had headed toward southeast Kansas on business or in hopes of staking a claim. Their families said that most of these men were carrying a fair amount of money.

A few newspapers ran stories based on the concerns of these families, but they were soon forgotten as local residents struggled through the challenges of life on the prairie in the 1870s. The beauty of the land and the independent, pioneering lifestyle were often accompanied by Mother Nature's less pleasant side. Searing heat, tornadoes, droughts, grasshopper invasions, and cold winter winds escorted by deadly ice and snow were then and continue today to be a part of the Kansas landscape.

It was hard on the human body and the human spirit, but Kate Bender developed a following and a bit of an income in promising to cure whatever ailed the people of the day. The flyers she posted claimed that she could "heal all sorts of Diseases," including blindness, fits, deafness, and dumbness. Original versions of these flyers are a part of the collection at the Kansas State Historical Society in Topeka. She called herself "Professor Katie Bender" but "professor" was certainly a loosely used adjective of the time, not reflecting any higher education or specialized training.

Among Kate's many talents was the ability to communicate with the dead through séances and similar means. People sought out those services somewhat regularly, according to tales associated with the Benders.

One story tells of a woman who couldn't pay for her treatments and exchanged her side saddle for Kate's healing powers. When the woman wasn't cured of her malady in a few weeks, she went to the Benders' inn to ask for the return of the saddle. Kate talked her into one more séance, but about halfway through, the woman got an uneasy feeling and decided to leave. The Bender men chased her into the prairie, where she hid in the tall prairie grass until they gave up their search.

She told a number of her neighbors that she had feared for her life that night, but most people didn't pay much attention to the woman's story. She had the reputation of being a bit of a flake and most people just laughed it off. The matter was soon forgotten by most who heard the tale.

LeRoy Dick was one of those neighbors who heard the story firsthand from the woman who lost her side saddle. As a township trustee, an elected position, he was as close to authority as was available in the community at the time.

Although he didn't entirely believe the woman's story that the Benders had been about to kill her, her experience did reinforce LeRoy's growing belief that the Benders were an odd lot. He had had a bit of a disagreement with the Benders about the number of cows they claimed on their property. As township trustee, it was LeRoy's responsibility to take a census of such matters.

He found it odd that so little farming was taking place on the two Bender claims, but the family seemed to have enough money to keep going. Maybe the little inn and the séance sideline brought in more business than anyone realized.

Two people who stopped at the inn for the night were George Longcohr and his little girl from the Independence area, about twenty miles away. George's wife had recently died and he was taking his daughter to stay with grandparents in Iowa until he could make the farm more productive and perhaps find a wife to help take care of the little girl. He had borrowed a team of horses and a wagon from Dr. William York to make the journey less of a hardship.

A few weeks later, Dr. York also left Independence to visit his parents near Fort Scott, a trip he made on a regular basis. While he was there, he heard people talking about an abandoned wagon and team of horses found nearby, now being cared for at a local livery. Out of curiosity, Dr. York went to check it out and was flabbergasted to see the very team and wagon he had loaned to his friend George Longcohr just a few weeks earlier.

By the early spring of 1873, the rumors about people going missing in southeast Kansas continued to escalate. Folks in those parts became indignant at the accusations that something was wrong in the community, and at the same time recognized that if they didn't do something to put the rumors to rest, it would reflect badly on their property values and the potential for businesses locating in the area.

A meeting was called to discuss the situation. They say more than one hundred people filled the tiny little schoolhouse on the prairie with much posturing and tough talk, but in the end, nobody really knew what to do or how to handle the problem.

It all came to a head when word got around that Dr. York had not returned to his family and practice in Independence. Dr. York's brother, Colonel Alexander York, a Civil War veteran and newly elected state senator in Kansas, took matters into his own hands by organizing a search party to scour the region.

They talked with a number of people, including LeRoy Dick, who all said they had their suspicions about the Bender family. The York party rode directly to the Bender inn and by all accounts had a very direct confrontation with Kate and Ma regarding the whereabouts of Dr. York. Not finding any answers, Colonel York and his colleagues continued their search elsewhere.

Another week or two passed. It was May 1, 1873, and spring was evident on the Kansas prairie. The wildflowers bloomed and crops began to grow as the sun warmed the soil.

Young Billy Toles, a neighbor to the Benders, passed their place on his way to Sunday church. He had wanted to talk to his neighbors about some of their cattle that had wandered onto his place in the past few days, but it looked as if no one was home.

On his way back from church, Billy stopped to look around. The house was closed up and none of the Benders were to be found. They had obviously been gone for more than a couple days, because the penned livestock were dead or dying from lack of food and water. The gruesome scene that Billy discovered was just the beginning of the wretched discoveries that would be made here in the next few days.

Word spread, and within twenty-four hours LeRoy Dick, the township trustee, was grappling with the magnitude of carnage while attempting to maintain order among the hundreds of people who came to witness what was unfolding in Labette County.

Anyone who had visited the Bender inn had commented on how filthy it was and of the ugly, stained curtain that divided the sleeping quarters from the eating/business area. As the day wore on, the activities at the inn over the past few years became clear.

Those who sat for a meal at the inn were directed to a seat with their backs to the curtain. While lovely Kate entertained and distracted the guest, either Pa or John or both would come from behind and club the unsuspecting guest in the head.

Their lifeless bodies would then drop through a trap door into a cellar, where they were laid out on a slab of rock and their throats slit ear to ear. Some bodies were mutilated and some dismembered, but the blows to the head and the slashed throats were the common factors.

Except the little girl.

As bodies were discovered buried in the soft, well-tended soil of the little orchard, all were naked and facedown in their shallow graves. But the little girl was found fully clothed on top of her father's body, where she had apparently been tossed and buried alive.

Dr. York's body was the first found. LeRoy Dick was devastated to discover the body of his wife's cousin, who had paid a visit about a year earlier. No one in the family had even noted that he was missing. One man was found buried in a well.

Not everyone was identified, and newspaper accounts vary between eight and eleven bodies being discovered in the next two days. Decomposed body parts were also found here and there. And then, of course, there were the bodies found out on the open prairie with skull fractures and throats slit more than two years before.

Three hammers confiscated at the scene and deemed to be the murder weapons are on display at the Cherryvale Museum. A very large, nasty-looking kitchen knife, also confiscated that day, is today in possession of the Kansas State Historical Society.

The Benders were nowhere to be found. Their wagon, an easily identifiable contraption with wheels more narrow in the front than in the back, was found abandoned near the train station in Thayer. Any doubt about the wagon's belonging to the Benders was erased when one of its floorboards was removed. On one side were the faded letters GROCRY. On the other side was the word GROCERIES.

Posses spread out across the country, and some say the Benders were quickly captured, hanged, and buried where they were found. That might have been in Oklahoma or Texas or Kansas, depending on whom you believe.

Others say they escaped and established a similar lifestyle near El Paso, Texas. Sightings of the Benders were reported in Colorado, Utah, Idaho, and even in Old Mexico.

LeRoy Dick became the local official most active in pursuing the Benders. Labette County spent thousands of dollars sending him and other investigators to track down leads in remote areas.

By 1889, sixteen years after the gruesome discoveries near Cherryvale, Kansas, the trail led to the logging communities of southeast Michigan, where two bawdy women had developed a vulgar reputation for marrying, fighting with, divorcing, and remarrying men in the logging camps. The women called themselves Almira Griffith and Sarah Eliza Davis.

However, Michigan authorities agreed there was enough evidence connecting these women to Ma and Kate Bender that LeRoy arrested them and brought them back to Oswego, Kansas, to face a jury. The preliminary hearing in November 1889 was a circus of witnesses and public speculation, well documented by newspapers from across the country, as to whether these were indeed the notorious Bender women.

As preparations for the trial were under way, the women's attorney uncovered paperwork identifying the woman believed to be Ma Bender as a woman who had been incarcerated in Michigan at the time of the murders. Such an alibi called for both women to be released from custody. The county bought them one-way train tickets out of town.

The people of Labette County were ready for the entire Bender episode to come to an end. But that was not to be the case.

Over the next fifty years, dozens more leads linked the Benders to crimes from coast to coast. Deathbed confessions were reported from numerous alleged posse members who admitted to tracking down the Benders within days of the evil discovery, killing them, and disposing of their bodies. But no one was ever able to confirm any of those stories.

So what happened to the four people who killed all of those innocent victims on the Kansas prairie? If the two women brought back to Labette County really were Ma and Kate, where did they go after they were released? And what about Pa and John?

Unfortunately, no one has those answers or will ever know the fate of the four known today as the Bloody Benders.

CHAPTER 2

The Frightful Childhood of Buffalo Bill Cody

Was Buffalo Bill Cody the heroic adventurer that history and popular media of the time tell us he was? Or was Bill Cody just a scared little boy who was thrust into the national spotlight based simply on his ability to survive amid difficult circumstances?

From the 1880s through the first two decades of the twentieth century, William Frederick Cody was the most famous entertainer in North America and perhaps the world. Better known as Buffalo Bill Cody, he was the Brad Pitt, George Clooney, and Johnny Depp of his time, all rolled into one and then some.

His Wild West shows visited thirteen countries and the forty-eight contiguous states on multiple occasions. He performed for and became friends with presidents, kings, and world leaders, including Pope Leo XIII. He was the subject of dime novels, comics, songs, and both silent and talkie movies. Buffalo Bill was the embodiment of the spirit of the American West, of the independence, self-sufficiency, and grandeur that appealed to those around the world who dreamed of America.

His shows portrayed and embellished his life as a Pony Express rider, army scout, buffalo hunter, and Indian fighter. He couldn't have been a more significant American hero if he had walked on the moon, stormed the beaches of Normandy, or liberated Baghdad. And he became a wealthy man because of it all.

But when Buffalo Bill and those shows came to Leavenworth, Kansas, which they did at least seven times, they never made any money. That's because Leavenworth was home to the Cody family and little Bill Cody gave away so many tickets to family, friends, and neighbors that the show was never profitable in his hometown.

He was welcomed in parades and eventually the community erected statues in his honor and named playgrounds, schools, and streets for him. For many years the people of Leavenworth held a weeklong festival carrying his name to honor the spirit of daring and adventure shared by the pioneer families who settled in this region, a spirit that was personified by Buffalo Bill himself.

However, the Leavenworth area had not always been so welcoming to the Codys. Little Bill was seven years old in 1854 when the family moved from LeClaire, Iowa, to the Kansas territory. Bill's older brother, Sam, had been killed in an accident with a horse, and his parents wanted a fresh start away from their grief. Plus, Bill's father, Isaac, had a brother who lived in Weston, Missouri, just across the Missouri River from Leavenworth. Any day now, the federal government was expected to open the Kansas and Nebraska territories to homesteaders, and the Codys wanted a head start in this exciting new land.

Bill Cody's flamboyant manner of dress later in life contributed to the legend that is Buffalo Bill Cody.

So the Cody family came to Kansas, a family that included Isaac and Mary, sisters Julia, Eliza, Laura, and May, and, of course, William. In May 1855 little brother Charlie was born into the family.

The Codys were not the only ones with their eyes on Kansas in 1854. In May of that year, Congress passed the Kansas-Nebraska Act, which basically stated that the issue of slavery in any new states coming into the Union would be decided by a vote of the people residing in those states. So those with strong emotions on both sides of the matter were moving to the region by the wagonload to influence the vote.

Things quickly became violent. Just across the river, Missouri was a slave state and "border ruffians" loudly protested those with opposing viewpoints who moved into the region. Homes and crops were burned; livestock and property were stolen; and men were hanged, stabbed, and shot for their beliefs. Many historians believe this period leading up to the Civil War, known as Bleeding Kansas, was more influential to the start of the war than the shots fired at Fort Sumter.

Politics had not motivated the Cody family to move to Kansas, yet they were immediately consumed by the hostility. Isaac Cody was not an abolitionist, but neither did he believe that slavery should be expanded in the United States and certainly not in his new home in Kansas.

It became impossible for anyone to remain neutral. There was no middle ground, and tolerance for opposing beliefs was not a part of the terrain. For the Cody family it all exploded one day when Isaac and little Bill were returning to their homestead just west of the fort when they were stopped by a proslavery crowd, whose members demanded that Isaac declare his position. When he did so, a man in the crowd leapt forward and stabbed Isaac in the back, just nicking his lung.

Bill witnessed the whole episode and feared for his own life as he helped his father back home.

The next day the crowd came to the Cody home to "finish what they had started." While Mary talked with the crowd downstairs, assuring them that her husband was not at home, Bill and his sister Julia positioned themselves upstairs in the bedroom where their father lay wounded. One held an ax, the other a shotgun, a fairly sobering and formidable task for children not yet in their teens.

As soon as he was physically able, Isaac left the family home, hiding in other communities where the free-state opinion dominated. At one point, the family received word that a mob was looking for Isaac, so little Bill, in bed with the flu, was sent to warn his father. The mob chased him until the scared little boy reached the safety of a friendly neighbor home. Bill was either so sick or so frightened that he had thrown up all over himself and his horse. The next day he continued his ride to warn his father.

For much of this time, the violence was directed only at the male head of the household. At that time, men were the only ones who could vote and therefore the only threat. But the brutality certainly affected everyone.

Almost everything of any value was stolen from the Codys, including their livestock and the crops on which they relied for food. At one point, a powder keg with a burned-out fuse was found under the porch, apparently placed there as the family slept inside.

This was the environment in which young Bill Cody was raised. His most impressionable years were filled with tension, stress, and vitriolic actions toward those he loved. At the same time, the stability and guidance that would have been provided in the daily presence of his father was missing.

However, Bill was a typical and rambunctious little boy, exploring the prairie on his pony, Prince, learning to shoot, idolizing the soldiers at Fort Leavenworth, and making friends with the Indians who still lived in the area. He didn't like school and attended with his sisters to appease his mother's wishes. He got into a schoolyard fight over a girl, and he fell in love with, then proposed marriage to his much older teacher. Dennis the Menace and Opie Taylor had nothing on this boy, and everyone thought well of Bill Cody.

Although young children of the 1860s typically had chores that would hobble the video-game mind-set of today's youth, it became necessary for young Bill to generate income to actually put food on the table and in the stomachs of his mother and siblings. He helped other farmers gather hay and earned a few dollars tracking down stray horses and livestock for the army.

When Isaac Cody finally returned to his family in Leavenworth, he was very ill and eventually died of perhaps the flu or pneumonia. He was buried on a hill not far from the family home on Pilot Knob Hill. Today that hill is known as Cody Hill, located on old Highway 73 in Leavenworth County.

So at the age of eleven, Bill was the man of the house. The freighting firm of Russell, Majors, and Waddell, based in Leavenworth, was leading wagon trains and supply trains west, so Bill signed on to work for the company at a salary of $40 per month. His job was to help with the animals and ride from the front to the back of the caravan delivering necessary messages. Although historians question some of the details, it was on this journey that Bill killed an Indian during an ambush on the wagon train.

In today's world of instant global communication, it's difficult to appreciate a time in our nation's history when mail delivery from the East Coast to California took a minimum of ten months. Although the railroads and telegraph were in the process of connecting the United States, the politicians in Washington, D.C., decided to authorize a remarkable short-term solution to the communication problem.

That solution was the Pony Express, and Buffalo Bill's employer, Russell, Majors, and Waddell, won the government contract to make it happen. Using a relay of mail carriers on horseback, the Pony Express delivered mail from St. Joseph, Missouri (the western terminus of the railroads at the time), to Sacramento, California, in ten days.

Now the problem with this phase of Bill's life and Old West history is that so few records were saved from the eighteen-month operation of the Pony Express. We know that Bill was not hired as one of the original scrawny fellows, but later when he joined the company at age fourteen, he was probably the youngest Pony Express rider.

The next claim, which became a significant story in the Buffalo Bill legend, not even the historians at the National Pony Express Museum in St. Joseph, Missouri, can verify. Because a couple of relief riders were not in place and Buffalo Bill was dedicated to the cause that "the mail should go through," he rode nonstop for twenty-two hours, covering at least 320 miles, making his the longest nonstop ride in Pony Express history.

Throughout this time and certainly after her husband's death, it would have been reasonable for Mary Cody to take her children back to Iowa or Ohio where her family lived, or anywhere away from the violence and painful memories of their father's death. However, Mary was undeniably stubborn. Her sympathies were with the Union and she was not about to allow anyone to tell her or her family where they could live. She stayed put and in her own way cast a vote to end slavery.

Bill wanted to enlist in the army, but his mother refused to allow it. She ran a little boardinghouse called the Valley Grove House and encouraged her children to get as much of an education as possible.

Instead, Mary's only son rode with a group that did as much or more damage to the Southern sympathizers in neighboring Missouri. Called the Red Legs, because of the identifying red bands worn around their thighs, this group has been referred

to by many historians as little more than a gang of thieves, burning, robbing, and stealing from the homes and communities
throughout Missouri. They openly brought their stolen loot
back to the streets of growing Leavenworth and sold them to the
highest bidder—thus earning a bit more income for the family.

Was Bill Cody finally getting vengeance for the trauma
rained on his family for so many years? Or was he doing what
was necessary for him and his family to survive? It's not a pretty
period, often glossed over in many accounts of his life, including
his autobiography, *The Life of Hon. William F. Cody, known as
Buffalo Bill, the famous hunter, scout and guide.*

The year 1864 was a turning point in the life of Bill Cody. As
the Civil War raged throughout the land, Bill and his sisters cared
for their mother, Mary, who was struggling with tuberculosis. She
died in November at age forty-seven and just a few weeks later, their
little brother Charlie also died. They were buried on Pilot Knob Hill
beside Isaac, although within a few years, the graves were lost to
time, a fact that greatly disturbed Bill in his adult years.

The war eventually ended and the nation's future was to
the West. The race was on to complete the railroads, and huge
teams of workers stretched across Nebraska, Wyoming, and
beyond. They needed to be fed. Bill shot buffalo faster than the
hordes of workers could consume the meat, and any criticism of
him was that so much meat was wasted.

Many historians consider that a sanitized version of the
story. Providing buffalo meat for railroad workers was only one

reason that Bill killed so many buffalo. At that time, killing buffalo and thus eliminating the primary food source of the Plains Indians was an accepted method of forcing the tribes to adhere to the demands of the federal government.

So is this where and how Buffalo Bill received his dubious nickname? It would make sense, and that's what most people believe.

Actually, Buffalo Bill was a fairly common nickname at that time. Among their ranks was a man named William Mathewson who lived near what is now Lyons, Kansas, on the Santa Fe Trail between 1859 and 1866. A part of his services to settlers in the region and travelers along the trail included offering water for humans and animals from a hand-dug well. Settlers likely would have starved to death during a severe drought in 1860 if not for the skills of Bill Mathewson in supplying buffalo meat. His charitable efforts earned him the nickname Buffalo Bill. Bill Cody worked for Bill Mathewson for a short while in 1866, and in later years as Cody's fame grew, Mathewson claimed that Cody had stolen the Buffalo Bill moniker.

As a point of interest, the hand-dug well near Lyons from which Bill Cody drank and drew water for his horse can still be visited today.

Another hunter by the name of Billy Comstock called himself Buffalo Bill and claimed to be the best buffalo hunter in the West. Sometime in 1868 near Sheridan, Kansas, Billy Comstock and Bill Cody had a shoot-out of sorts to determine who indeed was the best. The number of animals killed in this contest has been exaggerated beyond reality over the years, but in the end, Bill Cody won the title Buffalo Bill.

In the meantime, the Cody sisters continued to operate a little boardinghouse/hotel in Leavenworth and Bill explored the West, caught up for a while in the Colorado gold rush and serving as a scout for the US Army. He married Louisa Frederici of St. Louis and brought her to Leavenworth, where they had two children. Bill worked with and socialized with other such professionals of the day, including Wild Bill Hickok and General George Armstrong Custer.

Although the Cody family had been friends with Indians in Leavenworth, it became Bill's job to track and kill Indians. His skills in this field contributed to his notoriety and were of such caliber that he was awarded the Congressional Medal of Honor for bravery in a battle with the Sioux in which many soldiers and Indians were killed.

Followers of the Buffalo Bill legend often debate whether Bill enjoyed his work. The argument can be made that if you are indeed that good at your work, you must enjoy what you are doing. Others argue that it was just his job, a way to pay the bills.

Either way, an undisputable and macabre act of aggression and vengeance was after the death of Bill's friend George Custer at the Battle of the Little Bighorn in 1876. In his grief at losing his friend, Bill tracked down and killed the warrior who was believed at the time to have killed Custer. In his Wild West and other shows, Bill would ride through the arena with this scalp victoriously raised before a cheering audience.

Despite his unprecedented success, Bill accidently fell into show business in 1871 when he was asked to make a stage appearance in the Chicago performance of *Scouts of the Plains.* Some say he was an egotist who immediately fell in love with the applause and adoration of the crowd. Others say he simply saw the opportunity to make a lot of money and took advantage.

So for twenty-eight years, Buffalo Bill shared his version of the American West with audiences around the world, first in shows scripted by others, and then in his own productions. Much of the performance was based on his personal experience, and it's widely agreed that much of it became inflated over the years, not unlike Hollywood does today in making a story more intriguing for a viewing audience.

He brought his friends into the business, including Wild Bill Hickok, Annie Oakley, and even Sitting Bull. Bill became a champion of American Indian rights and even worked to preserve the buffalo whose population he so gloriously decimated.

While visiting his sister May in Denver, Buffalo Bill died on January 10, 1917. He is buried on Lookout Mountain near the city of Golden. It is undisputed that William F. Cody lived a remarkable life in an uncertain and difficult time in American history. But the question remains: Did he accomplish all of this because he truly was a hero, or was he just a scared little boy whose motivations to provide for those around him followed him into adulthood and the pages of American history?

CHAPTER 3

The Dalton Gang's Buried Treasure

H ad the Dalton Gang not died on the streets of Coffeyville, Kansas, that October day in 1892, would they have become more famous than the Jesse James Gang? Who were they trying to impress? And did they really leave a fortune buried along the banks of Onion Creek on the Kansas-Oklahoma border?

No one ever said that life was easy on the Kansas prairie in the first couple of decades after the Civil War. Work was back-breakingly hard and without end for those who came to the region with the dream of establishing homes and communities. Mother Nature provided enough of a challenge with droughts, tornadoes, and grasshopper plagues. Medical care was almost nonexistent, along with most of the very basic amenities of life.

The American Indians had just about given up the fight for their native lands, leaving newcomers to the region an even greater threat from the less-than-civilized Anglo-Americans who preyed upon the honest, hardworking homesteaders and settlers.

A small-time group of hooligans who called themselves the Dalton Gang caused a bit of trouble along the Kansas-Oklahoma border in the 1890s but didn't make too many headlines. They stole a few horses, rustled a cow or two, and robbed a couple of trains. The gang was made up of Bob, Gratton, and Emmett Dalton along with Dick Broadwell, Bill Doolin, and Bill Power.

The Daltons don't necessarily stand out because they were successful in the business of stealing from others and making other people's life more difficult. They stand out because of their audacity and hubris, along with a pretty good dose of stupidity.

The Daltons are also notable because they had been the good guys, on the side of the law that tracked down horse thieves, cattle rustlers, and train robbers. So what went wrong? What pushed three Dalton brothers into a life of crime that ultimately resulted in their own deaths and serious injury as well as that of six others on the streets of Coffeyville, the very town they called home?

Twenty-first-century pundits would, of course, first look at their parents, probably blaming them for creating a home environment that contributed to the boys' poor choices in friends and activities.

But don't blame Louis and Adeline Dalton. The couple married in Jackson County, Missouri, in 1851 and eventually had fifteen children together, ten boys and five girls. The family moved around the area quite a bit in an attempt to escape much of the violence in the area before the start of the Civil War. They

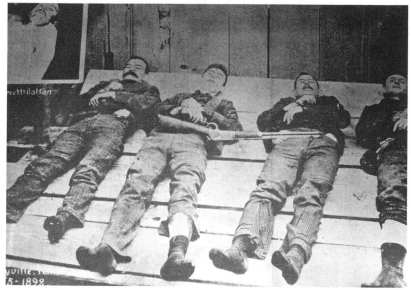

Death photo of the Dalton Gang on display at Dalton Defenders Museum in Coffeyville.

made sure that all fifteen of their children went to school long enough to learn to read and write.

However, it's certainly worth noting that prior to her marriage, Adeline Dalton was Adeline Younger, as in the Cole Younger Gang, second cousins to Jesse and Frank James, as in the James-Younger Gang. Adeline was Cole and Bob Younger's aunt.

Okay, well, maybe there can be some finger-pointing at the family tree in this particular scenario.

After Adeline married and began having children of her own, who knows how often or if ever her sons met Cole Younger. It's possible the Dalton children even met Jesse and Frank James at some point in their young lives. Years later, Frank James and

Emmett Dalton would go into a legitimate, albeit unsuccessful business together, but in their formative years, it's hard to say what influence the illegal antics of the James and Younger families had on the Daltons.

As much as anywhere else, Coffeyville was home for the Dalton family. Louis is buried near here, as is the eldest son, Frank. Later, Grat and Bob also found their final resting place in the soil of Coffey County.

That Louis and Adeline did their best with their children was evident in the chosen career of their first child, Frank. For three years, from 1885 to 1887, he was a US deputy marshal out of Fort Smith, Arkansas. He tangled with some of the toughest bad guys in the territory until he was killed in the line of duty in November 1887.

The legendary "hanging judge" Isaac Parker of Fort Smith asked that Grat and Bob fill their elder brother's shoes by tracking down ruffians in Indian Territory. The brothers accepted badges and worked in that capacity for the better part of two years.

There's something to be said here about the role of law enforcement in the Old West in the latter part of the nineteenth century. Although town sheriffs and US marshals and their deputies were highly valued members of the community who were expected to put their lives on the line when needed, they just weren't paid that well. Like others, the Dalton brothers did their jobs to the best of their abilities, but their paychecks were insufficient as well as sporadic.

Despite their Methodist-Episcopal upbringing and Adeline's best efforts, temptation soon got the better of Grat and
Bob. They stole a few horses, sold illegal whiskey, and openly
confiscated whatever items they felt served their needs. Bob and
Grat were lucky indeed that they were not prosecuted for their
actions. Instead, they were dismissed for "conduct unbecoming
to law enforcement."

In the meantime, their sister Eva had married and moved
with her husband, John Whipple, to Meade, Kansas, where he
operated a business and they built a small but pleasant home
with a barn and necessary outbuildings nearby.

The Oklahoma Territory had opened for white settlement
and Adeline had moved with some of the youngest children to a
homestead near Kingfisher, Oklahoma. Louis continued to operate his horse-trading business out of Coffeyville but died there of
pneumonia in 1890.

By the beginning of the last decade of the nineteenth century, Grat, who was almost thirty years old, and Bob, who was
twenty-five, were unemployed, but certainly not without means.
Along with their youngest brother, Emmett, who was not yet
twenty-one, they began riding with three men named Bill Doolin, Bill Power, and Dick Broadwell. Occasionally a few other
wannabe outlaws rode with the gang, but the basis of the Dalton
Gang was these six men.

Cattle rustling, horse thieving, and other petty thefts satisfied the gang only for so long. They had expensive tastes and

burned through money as fast as they could steal it. When they died, the Daltons left a big debt at a menswear shop in Coffeyville for everything from silk handkerchiefs to multiple sets of underwear. The saddle Bob Dalton rode into town on that last morning of his life, now on display at the Dalton Defenders Museum in Coffeyville, was extremely well-made, ornamented with extravagant fringe and silver studs in the shape of hearts.

So the Daltons cranked it up a notch or two, adding train robbery to their portfolio of criminal expertise. Maybe they were smart, or maybe they were lazy, but instead of chasing a moving train on horseback, the Daltons waited until the train pulled into the station, usually in very small communities, before attempting to rob it.

Having taken what they could from the passengers and freight cars, they would make a couple of passes through town on horseback, whooping and shooting it up. It seems they wanted people to know exactly who they were and what they had just done. It was after a train robbery in Adair, Oklahoma, while shooting up the town that the Daltons killed their first person. A doctor hiding indoors in a pharmacy was hit by a stray bullet and died of his wounds.

That moved the Dalton Gang way up the list of the region's most wanted outlaws. The gang disappeared to Colorado and California for a while, but years later, it became very apparent that they had spent some time with their sister Eva Whipple in Meade.

The small, inviting home that still stands today in its original location at the corner of Pearlette and Green Streets had, at some time, been equipped with a tunnel that ran ninety-five feet between the house and the barn. It's not inconceivable in those days that property owners might have developed some sort of protection from the elements between the house and the barn to care for their livestock during inclement weather.

However, if the tunnel was built for such innocuous purposes, why is it that one end was hidden behind a movable shelf in the kitchen pantry and the other end was under a platform where bags of feed were stacked?

Shortly before the big shoot-out in Coffeyville, Eva and her husband, John, moved from Meade, leaving no forwarding address or any information as to their whereabouts. The cute little house was eventually sold for back taxes to the Marshall family. Years later, one of the Marshall daughters wrote of the occasional surprises the family received when unexpected "guests" would arrive via the pantry rather than the front door.

By the early 1890s, Jesse James had been dead for about eight years. The famous and disastrous attempted robbery of a bank in Northfield, Minnesota, which had devastated the James-Younger Gang, was almost fifteen years in the past. But it weighed heavily on the Dalton Gang.

Jesse James's name was known around the world. For many, he was not an outlaw at all, but a martyr of the South and a decent family man. His death had made him even more famous, and it was the fame that the Dalton Gang really wanted.

Although Grat was the oldest of the surviving Dalton children, many agreed that he was definitely not the brightest. Bob was the brains of the group, and young Emmett, not yet twenty-one years old, idolized both of his big brothers.

So it was probably Bob who came up with the idea to rob two banks simultaneously in the same town—a feat that had never been done before, even by the great Jesse and Frank James. The outlaws on the Younger side of the family would certainly have to hold Aunt Adeline's children in greater esteem if they pulled off such a caper.

Bob Dalton knew just the perfect town and knew it pretty well: Coffeyville. Although they hadn't been back to town for almost two years, they knew there were two banks almost right across the street from each other. The Condon & Company Bank, now on the National Register of Historic Places, and the First National Bank perfectly fit their plan.

The timing was perfect as well. In early October, most of the crops had been harvested and the area farmers had deposited the money in the banks. Later it was determined that each bank held about $20,000 in gold and silver on the morning of October 5.

So the Dalton Gang set out for Coffeyville, but not before getting their hands on a few fake beards and mustaches to use as disguises. Although it had been some time since any of the

Daltons had been seen on the streets of Coffeyville, now that their reputation was getting around as bank and train robbers, they didn't want anyone to be tipped off as they rode into town.

On the night of October 4, 1892, they camped about four miles south of town on the banks of Onion Creek where it flows into the Verdigris River. Emmett reported later that someone suggested they send one or two of the gang into town the next day to scout things out. But the idea was nixed, probably by Bob, since he was the brains of the group.

A number of historians and trivia buffs who have spent a significant amount of time and energy studying these types of things believe that the outlaws might have been carrying anywhere between $10,000 and $20,000 in gold and silver from previous illegal activities when they stopped at Onion Creek. Many of these same historians and history buffs believe the Dalton Gang, anticipating that they would return late the next morning and obviously wanting to travel as light as possible out of Coffeyville, buried all of that gold and silver somewhere around their campsite.

That was the extent of planning the Daltons executed before attempting the great feat that would elevate their name above the James name in the lore and esteem of Old West outlaws.

In the twenty-first century, travelers are often alerted to road closures, street repairs, and other traffic concerns via any number of media. But on this Wednesday morning in October 1892, the six men camped at Onion Creek had no idea that a little street repair was under way in Coffeyville. Basically, the streets were being graded, and improved drainage ditches were being cut alongside the elevated wooden sidewalks. As a result, the hitching posts that were fundamental to doing business in any town of that time period had been temporarily removed.

If the Daltons had waited another day and sent someone into town, they would have immediately realized they had a problem. Where would they park the getaway car? Or in this case, where would they tie their horses so they could quickly disappear in a cloud of dust?

So they headed to town with the plans for Grat Dalton, Bill Power, and Dick Broadwell to take the Condon Bank. Bob and Emmett Dalton, along with Bill Doolin, would take the First National Bank. However, about halfway into town, Bill Doolin's horse went lame, so he turned around and went back to the campsite to care for his horse and wait for the others.

This left five members of the gang to ride into town together, but many on the streets of Coffeyville later swore they saw six men arrive together. If so, who was that sixth man and how did he escape unharmed? Where did he go?

The next question is this: When the Daltons realized the hitching posts were gone, why didn't they just turn around and wait a few more days? Arrogance or ignorance is the likely answer to that question. Impatience and hubris also probably played a part in that fatal mistake, but, by then, their adrenaline was pumping and turning back might never have entered anyone's mind.

It was about nine a.m. as the five entered town, each with Colt six-shooters in their holsters and Winchester rifles in their hands. The closest hitching posts they could find were in a narrow alley off of Walnut Street, a good two blocks from the First National Bank doorway.

Somewhere along the way, either as they rode into town or as they walked the short distance to the banks, someone recognized one of the Daltons. It was probably a pharmacist named Alex McKenna, who was sweeping outside his business that morning. Whoever first saw them, within five minutes, the word had quietly yet dramatically spread that the Daltons were in town and were robbing both banks.

Despite the images left by Hollywood over the years, not everyone in the Old West carried a gun at all times. Therefore, the citizens on the street that morning quickly converged on Isham's Hardware, next door to the First National Bank, grabbing the guns and ammunition they would need to defend their town.

Bob and Emmett Dalton entered the First National Bank and all went according to plan. Grat Dalton, Bill Power, and Dick Broadwell entered the Condon Bank and immediately grabbed $3,000 in silver coins from the teller. However, the banker told them the safe was on a time lock and wouldn't open for fifteen more minutes. Grat decided they could wait, another stupid decision.

By this time, the town was fully armed and in place behind wagons and barrels and high on rooftops. They started blasting through the windows of the Condon Bank. Emmett and Bob were just coming out of the First National Bank, so they turned around, exited through the bank's back door, and ran two blocks toward the horses, killing at least two men on their way.

Using hostages as shields, Grat, Bill, and Dick fought their way out of the Condon Bank and started running down the alley toward the horses, dropping silver coins as they ran.

Dick Broadwell is the only one who actually made it onto his horse and out of the alley. Just as he was making it out of town, he fell off his horse, dead of his wounds. Grat, Bob, and Bill died there in the alley along with Sheriff Charles Connelly. Emmett Dalton fell with his brothers, his body blistered by twenty-three bullet holes, but he lived.

It lasted less than fifteen minutes. Four citizens of Coffeyville were dead, along with the outlaws, and a dozen or so more were injured. But they had stopped the attempted robbery of two banks that would have stripped the hardworking, honest residents of Coffeyville of more than $40,000. In so doing, they had also taken the lives of four villainous criminals, perhaps saving other communities from similar fates.

As the bodies were examined and photographed, more than $900 in cash was found on Bob Dalton. His brother Grat was carrying about $75 and wearing a beautiful diamond ring and expensive gold watch, additional proof of their extravagant lifestyle.

So what happened to that gold and silver buried on Onion Creek? Bill Doolin was found waiting there along with other gear, but not a penny of the money. Was Bill Doolin the sixth figure that some people reported riding to town that morning? Or was it someone else who escaped into oblivion before the shooting started?

These questions and more were surely asked of Emmett Dalton as he recovered from his wounds and stood trial for his crimes, but either he never knew or never gave up the answer. Maybe there was no gold buried along the creek at all, making it just another of the hundreds of unanswered mysteries of Kansas.

CHAPTER 4

Nicodemus, Kansas: Legendary Black Town of the American West

What makes a tiny little town of just twenty-nine mostly elderly residents, barely a speck on the map of northwest Kansas, worthy of national attention? And how is it that the entire country is better because of what has taken place here?

One doesn't often stumble upon Nicodemus, Kansas, by accident. You really have to be looking for it. Located thirty-five miles north of the swath that Interstate 70 cuts through the state and about forty miles south of the Nebraska border in Graham County—among the ten least populated counties of the 105 in the state—Nicodemus has seen better days.

In the history of the Old West, an endless number of towns were founded with the hopeful vision of grand metropolises flourishing on the prairie. An equally endless number have disappeared over the years, many not even receiving the status of ghost town or a historical marker identifying where these dreams died. So what is it about Nicodemus that has kept it alive for almost 140 years?

All Colored People

THAT WANT TO

GO TO KANSAS,

On September 5th, 1877,

Can do so for $5.00

IMMIGRATION.

WHEREAS, We, the colored people of Lexington, Ky,. knowing that there is an abundance of choice lands now belonging to the Government, have assembled ourselves together for the purpose of locating on said lands. Therefore,

BE IT RESOLVED, That we do now organize ourselves into a Colony, as follows:— Any person wishing to become a member of this Colony can do so by paying the sum of one dollar ($1.00), and this money is to be paid by the first of September, 1877, in instalments of twenty-five cents at a time, or otherwise as may be desired.

RESOLVED, That this Colony has agreed to consolidate itself with the Nicodemus Towns, Solomon Valley, Graham County, Kansas, and can only do so by entering the vacant lands now in their midst, which costs $5.00.

RESOLVED, That this Colony shall consist of seven officers—President, Vice-President, Secretary, Treasurer, and three Trustees. President—M. M. Bell; Vice-President —Isaac Talbott; Secretary—W. J. Niles; Treasurer—Daniel Clarke; Trustees—Jerry Lee, William Jones, and Abner Webster.

RESOLVED, That this Colony shall have from one to two hundred militia, more or less, as the case may require, to keep peace and order, and any member failing to pay in his dues, as aforesaid, or failing to comply with the above rules in any particular, will not be recognized or protected by the Colony.

This type of flyer was widely circulated throughout the South, encouraging freed slaves to come to Kansas.

The answer begins before the Civil War, before there was a state called Kansas.

It was 1854 and the Kansas and Nebraska territories had just been opened for white settlement. The Kansas-Nebraska Act included the provision that the issue of slavery would be decided by a vote of the state's residents. This obviously made a few headlines in the newspapers of the time. As a result, passionate individuals who supported and abhorred the concept of slavery headed to the soon-to-be states.

Because neighboring Missouri was already a slave state, things became fairly ugly on the Kansas border. Homes and crops were burned, men were murdered, women and children were threatened. In August 1863, the town of Lawrence was raided by a gang of Missouri ruffians led by William Quantrill. At least 150 men died as the town burned to the ground.

Those years were so violent they became known as Bleeding Kansas. Yet, on January 29, 1861, just before the start of the Civil War, Kansas was admitted to the Union as a free state. Nebraska soon followed.

In the meantime, Congress passed the Homestead Act of 1862, basically giving away *free* land to anyone who would break ground, build a house, live there, plant crops, and otherwise stick with it for five years. Kansas was one of thirty states opened for homesteading.

When the Civil War ended in 1865, the slaves were emancipated and filled with the hope and optimism that is synonymous with freedom. However, after a few years, the realities of Reconstruction, racial divisions, the Ku Klux Klan, and so much more began to sink in. Many Southern whites who tried to provide education and other opportunities for blacks were harassed or murdered right along with those they were trying to help. In places like Mississippi, laws were passed that prevented African Americans from buying land and whites from leasing or deeding land to former slaves.

Kansas, however, was out there, a place where slavery had never been permitted. "The Promised Land" it was called by Governor George Anthony and others who believed that after all the people of Kansas had been through to guarantee freedom during Bleeding Kansas, they were obligated to encourage the former slaves to find a safe home here.

Throughout the South, handbills and posters called for "all colored people that want to go to Kansas" to assemble at various times and places. For about $5 per person, land companies formed with the intent of leading former slaves to the Promised Land.

And yet a young pioneering former slave named William Smith didn't wait for the group migration that would later take place. As soon as possible after he was freed near Paducah, Kentucky, he had headed west and was already established as a homesteader in Kansas.

Sometime in early 1877, a white land speculator named William Hill approached Smith with the idea of starting a town for disenfranchised former slaves. The two started searching for an area large enough to accommodate homesteading claims and a town site for several hundred families.

One story told is that during their explorations, Hill sat down to rest one day and was frightened by a huge snake. That's about the time they decided they had looked long enough. On June 8, 1877, they registered the town site with the Federal Land Office.

In Topeka they became acquainted with four African-American ministers who represented a colony of about 350 former slaves in the communities around Lexington, Kentucky. Smith, Hill, and the ministers quickly worked through the details and officially formed the Nicodemus Town Company.

In selecting the name Nicodemus for their new home, the former slaves received inspiration from the song "Wake Nicodemus," which tells of an African prince named Nicodemus who was captured by slave traders and came to America on the first slave ship. Upon his death, he was said to have made those around him promise to wake him up in time for the jubilee, which was known among slaves as the time they would again be free. A particularly moving line in the song, which is attributed to the naming of the town, is "the good times a-comin' is almost here; it was long, long, long on the way." So, along with Smith and Hill, the four ministers returned to Kentucky in search of former slaves willing to leave the South behind and establish a new life in Kansas, in a new town called Nicodemus. In September of that year, about 350 free blacks left Lexington, Kentucky, by train, headed to the Promised Land.

Later these people would be known as Exodusters, but the massive exodus from the South didn't really begin until 1879. It's generally agreed that most Exodusters were from Tennessee, Mississippi, Louisiana, and Texas and left as individuals, not a large group, and not with the intent of founding a town of their own. The group from Kentucky was composed of true pioneers in a movement that would change the face of the South and the landscape of the American West.

Tom Johnson was one of the former slaves who made that journey in September 1877 with his wife and three children. Johnson and the others knew nothing about Bleeding Kansas. In fact, they knew nothing about Kansas at all, except that it was free. Most of these former slaves had probably never been very far off of their plantations, if at all, prior to emancipation. The South was all they had known.

The train ride took three days to reach Ellis, Kansas, thirty-five miles south of the future town site of Nicodemus. These black pioneers had very little money, no horses, and no wagons. They had to walk for two days, carrying their very few possessions, to reach their little slice of the Promised Land.

To say that they were a bit disappointed had to have been an understatement. Western Kansas is predominantly treeless and almost constantly ravaged by wind. At that time in history, others had called it the American Desert.

About sixty in the group took a look around and got back on the train to the familiarity of Kentucky, complete with the

KKK, Jim Crow laws, limited prospects for advancement, and certainly a limited experience in freedom.

Tom Johnson and his family stayed. They, along with the others, soon realized the disastrous timing of their arrival. Winter was coming and winter on the Great Plains is much more harsh than in the hills of Kentucky. They had no shelter, very few tools, and limited natural resources with which to build shelter.

It was too late to plant a garden and the landscape provided no wild fruits or much else to eat. They certainly had no guns to shoot antelope or other wildlife for food. They had no cows, no chickens, or any other livestock. And winter's brutality was fast approaching.

Despite the widely held perception that Kansas is as flat as a pancake, that's just not true, and certainly not along the banks of the Solomon River in the northwest part of the state. The landscape cannot be called hilly or mountainous by any stretch of the imagination, but it does have a rolling quality to it with abbreviated escarpments and small limestone bluffs along the river.

That's where these first residents of Nicodemus found the shelter they desperately needed. By sharing their limited tools and probably making a few more primitive tools, they began digging holes in the hillsides to create dugouts, a form of shelter that was actually very common for homesteaders throughout the Great Plains and for centuries before in military conflicts throughout Europe.

By creating a hole in the top for smoke from a fire to escape and by creating a doorway, covered by a blanket or some natural material, a dugout could provide a fairly decent shelter for humans and animals. One well-maintained dugout remains today a few miles east of Nicodemus along Highway 24, but its particular purpose was another unpleasant aspect of the settlers' new life in the Promised Land.

The men made slingshots and clubs and did their best to trap a few jackrabbits and other wild game. They were occasionally lucky enough to knock an occasional antelope in the head or a few birds from the sky. Before it got too cold, they fished in the Solomon River. They struggled daily for enough food for the moment while attempting to set aside something for the upcoming winter.

The buffalo, which had served as a primary source of food and warmth for the American Indians for generations, were long gone, but their skeletons littered the prairie like tumbleweeds. Men, women, and children collected buffalo bones, which they were able to sell for use in fertilizer production back east.

Some men were able to find paid work with the few established white farmers in the region. Others were employed by the Kansas-Pacific Railroad at Ellis, thirty-five miles from Nicodemus. With that little bit of cash, the first settlers could buy warmer clothing and a few supplies, and somehow they survived that first winter.

Those long cold days and colder nights surely gave plenty of time for reflection on what their new freedom and land ownership meant to these very special pioneers. They gathered together in prayer, asking for strength to overcome the new challenges before them in this, their Promised Land. The first Christmas on the prairie was celebrated with tumbleweeds as Christmas trees and probably very little else to distinguish it from any other day, except for the faith celebrated in each little dugout.

One event that was cause for significant celebration was the birth of Tom Johnson's grandson, Henry Williams, the first baby born in Nicodemus. He was soon joined by a brother, Charles, and other babies. A school would soon be needed. Mr. and Mrs. Z. T. Fletcher began the school system in their dugout in 1879. In 1887 a four-room school building became the educational home for the young people of Nicodemus who would eventually make great contributions to the state and to the American people.

The next black emigrants from Kentucky were in a smaller group of about sixty people. They arrived in Nicodemus in the spring of 1878, also by train and also walking two days to the town site. However, they were a little better prepared, bringing more supplies and a bit more money.

Several ministers, both black and white, asked white farmers in the area to loan a team of mules or oxen for a few days at a time to help break ground. That helped with the backbreaking necessary chores but did little to improve relations between blacks and whites.

However, local newspapers of the day kept up on the developments of Nicodemus. One story reported on a black farmer who, with one cow and his wife, broke twelve acres of new sod and cultivated eight acres of corn in one season. Another built a four-foot-high hedgerow around 160 acres using only a spade. Any farmer of that period or any time since could not help but admire the energy and fortitude required to accomplish such chores.

However, admiration went only so far in the 1880s. Access to many of the basic supplies needed for survival on the plains required a visit to nearby towns. Most of the time these journeys were made on foot, although by this time a few teams of horses and mules were a part of the growing Nicodemus community.

The challenge, however, was not so much getting to nearby towns, but getting out of those towns by sundown.

Despite the extensive campaign by elected leaders and everyday citizens of Kansas to attract Southern blacks to Kansas, there still existed a significant amount of racism. Many towns in the state, including nearby Stockton and Hays, where the residents of Nicodemus would go for supplies, were called "sundowner towns."

Basically African Americans were encouraged to come to town and spend their money or work in menial jobs, but they were not allowed to live in town or even spend the night. They were allowed in only during the daylight hours and told to be out by sundown.

Therefore, more communal dugouts were built just a mile or two outside these towns so that those traveling from the Nicodemus community would have some shelter for the night. One of those dugouts remains in very good condition just two miles west of Stockton on Highway 24 en route to Nicodemus.

The last group of about fifty people came to Nicodemus in the spring of 1879. These former slaves had been living near Leavenworth after the war, but many had ties to Kentucky in one way or another. They knew of the potential in Nicodemus and wanted to be a part of it.

The journey by wagon from Leavenworth to Nicodemus took about a week and their arrival was a welcome one in the little community. Along with the sporadic arrival of other black families who were officially a part of the Exoduster movement, the population in town grew to 650. Before long, two churches and a little hotel had been built.

At its height, Nicodemus offered two newspapers, a post office, grocery and hardware stores, schools, churches, a bank, and a baseball team for its residents and area farm families. It was a premier example of an African-American community and exemplified what their freedom allowed. It was a typically American community.

Residents began to build above ground, usually in what was called a soddy. Relying on square chunks of sod, held firmly together by the roots of prairie grass, sod homes were almost as solid as brick homes. The first building of native limestone was built in Nicodemus in 1880.

However, like many agricultural communities, Nicodemus relied heavily on the railroads to send the harvest to market in the East. The Missouri Pacific and the Union Pacific bypassed all of Graham County in 1887 and 1888, respectively. As a result, many residents gave up on Nicodemus and moved their homes, businesses, and futures to communities with greater prospects.

Missing out on the railroads was the death knell for towns throughout the Great Plains, particularly those established by African Americans after the Civil War. Nicodemus was the first town west of the Mississippi built by and for black settlers, and today it remains the last.

Although the lack of a railroad knocked the wind out of Nicodemus's growth, the pioneering spirit of the people of the community continued to thrive. In a sense, the isolation created a cohesive spirit of determination that resonates in their descendants today.

Farmers expanded their land ownership and production capabilities. They survived the Great Depression and the Dust Bowl, continuing to succeed in the face of all odds. They built churches and schools, raised families, and sent their children to college.

While some will argue that the railroad caused Nicodemus's population decline, another reality is that, after a generation or two, everyone in Nicodemus was related to everyone else in town. If young people were to marry, they often found their spouses elsewhere. Although some came back home to farm and to raise families, many found opportunities outside of the little town on Highway 24.

Therefore, the descendants of Nicodemus settlers are spread far and wide, many making great contributions to the communities in which they live, in their chosen professions, and, as a result, to their states and country.

The first African American elected to a state office in Kansas came from Nicodemus. E. P. McCabe served two terms as state auditor between 1883 and 1887. George Washington Jones and W. L. Sayers became county attorneys. Others went on to contribute to every profession from education and journalism to medicine and law. A number of the Buffalo Soldiers, members of the 10th Cavalry regiment so nicknamed by American Indians, came from within the Nicodemus community. Professional athletes, entertainers, and business owners often have direct ties to Nicodemus.

Among those are Veryl Switzer of the Green Bay Packers and Gerald Willhite of the Denver Broncos. The great Gale Sayers of the Chicago Bears is a descendant of Nicodemus settlers.

Cooper Bates, who had a recurring role for years on *Days of Our Lives,* is a descendant of these first settlers. Loretta Long, who has played Susan Robinson on *Sesame Street* since its inception, traces her family tree to those first settlers in Nicodemus.

As a result of tireless efforts of a few dedicated community members and the African-American Institute for Historic Preservation, the town's unique story was brought to the attention of leading members of the US Congress. Kansas Senators Bob Dole and James Pearson introduced legislation that paved the way for five of the oldest buildings in Nicodemus to become a National Historic Landmark District. The legislation became law in January 1976.

Twenty years later, in November 1996, the little town became a unit of the National Park Service dedicated to telling the story of these pioneers who accomplished so much with so little, surviving the odds with a spirit not unlike that of the *Mayflower* Pilgrims who, with a dream of freedom from persecution, helped build a great nation.

So, what if the railroad had come through Nicodemus? And later an interstate? The community might have flourished; indeed it might have become a metropolis on the prairie. But what would have been lost? Would the cohesiveness and fortitude of its citizens been diminished as well as the identity of this unique community? And then what story would be left to tell?

CHAPTER 5

The Phog That Blankets
Lawrence, Kansas

How would basketball have evolved differently if James Naismith, the inventor of the game, had taken a job anywhere other than at the University of Kansas? And if he had, would there still be a sixth man on the court of KU home games today?

Allen Field House at the University of Kansas is a barn of an old building. Built in 1955, there's nothing really pretty about this building on the west side of the KU campus. It's just a big old limestone structure with no particularly intriguing or appealing architectural elements. It just sits there, rooted like an indelible force of nature in the unflinching Kansas prairie.

Once you're inside Allen Field House, however, something magical happens that is more miraculous than Dorothy Gale and her house flying over the rainbow. But this is not fiction or a Hollywood movie set. This is Kansas basketball.

On game night, any game night, every seat in the 17,000-capacity arena is filled. The idea of a basketball game at KU not being sold out is preposterous. With the exception of a few supporters of the visiting team who stand out, everyone is decked out in those patented shades of vivid blue, brilliant yellow, and crisp red. They chant and *whooooosh* and stomp their feet until the old barn's rafters and windows quiver in an attempt to accommodate the overpowering energy from within.

The actual court on which the game is played inside Allen Field House is polished and as protected and revered here as if it were an original copy of the Declaration of Independence. That analogy is not an exaggeration, because, really, few images are more authentically American than a driveway basketball goal or a neighborhood court filled with friends of all ages gathered to shoot hoops. The court at the University of Kansas is named for the man who, in this scenario, wrote the basketball equivalent of the Declaration of Independence—i.e., the rules of the game.

His name, of course, was James Naismith. However, James Naismith was not an American. He was a Canadian high school dropout and lumberjack, an orphan of Scottish immigrants, and a devout Presbyterian. Of course, he later returned to high school and college, received a degree in theology as well as a medical degree, and in 1923 became a naturalized American citizen.

It was Naismith's unwavering belief in the connection between the condition of the human body and the human soul that resulted in the creation of a game—an activity, he called it—that is second only to soccer as the world's most popular sport.

The story is well known of Naismith's assignment as a physical education student at the Springfield, Massachusetts, YMCA in 1891 to create an indoor physical activity to keep students fit during the long winter months. He nailed two peach baskets to the ten-foot-high rafters of the gymnasium and composed thirteen rules to guide the game.

However, some contend that Naismith didn't really write those rules all by himself. Some even say that basketball was first played in a YMCA in Herkimer, Massachusetts, not Springfield, but no one in Kansas gives any credence to those ideas.

It's likely that Naismith, in fulfilling his assignment, collaborated with other students and athletic directors in the area, brainstorming for ideas and asking for feedback on his activity. But the family of Lambert Will contends that it was more than that. They say that Lambert Will actually wrote the rule about passing the ball across the court. They say that Naismith's plan was for the ball to roll across the floor. And according to the Will family legacy, Lambert was the one who told Naismith to cut the bottoms out of the peach baskets to allow the game to move faster. They also credit Lambert's wife, Mary, with crocheting the very first basketball net.

Again, nobody in Kansas buys that theory—a fantasy, they call it in Lawrence, where the original thirteen typewritten rules are protected behind glass (much like the Declaration of Independence) in the Booth Family Hall of Athletics at the University of Kansas. But still, look closely at the bottom of the

James Naismith
on the University of
Kansas campus.

Phog Allen at the field house that bears his
name in Lawrence.

second page. There's clearly a smudge where Naismith or some-one changed the date from February 1892 to December 1891.

Either way, Naismith left Massachusetts in 1895 to continue his work at the YMCA in Denver and attend medical school at the University of Colorado. In 1898, at age thirty-six, Naismith and his family, which included wife Maude and three daughters, moved to Lawrence so James could become the university's first physical education instructor and director of the chapel.

There he organized the first basketball team, which would eventually become the Rock Chalk Jayhawks. It's not known whether he had other job offers, but if he had gone elsewhere, would the Jayhawks have become the basketball superpower they are today? Or would they be just like any other college team out there, hoping to find their name in one of the opening brackets of the NCAA tournament each March, maybe occasionally mak-ing it into the Sweet Sixteen? Would even one championship banner now hang in Allen Field House?

Unlike the fans of his game, particularly those Rock Chalk fans at KU, Naismith never got too excited about basketball. He certainly recognized its popularity, but he appreciated it more as a physical activity than as a game of any kind. He thought the players' speed and agility and the overall physical conditioning were more important than scoring points. Triumph over another team was irrelevant.

Such an attitude correlated directly with his 55–60 career as a coach—the only losing record in the history of KU basketball.

But that never concerned Naismith. As he later told an emerging powerhouse in the game, "You can't coach basketball. You just play it."

One of Naismith's students was a young man named Pete Allen, one of six brothers from Independence, Missouri, with quite a reputation for their athletic prowess in everything from football and baseball to tennis and rugby. The Allen brothers had their own basketball team, playing competitively throughout western Missouri and eastern Kansas. They regularly beat the fledgling teams at the University of Missouri and the University of Kansas.

Pete's younger brother, Forrest, visited him in Lawrence and learned to appreciate the progressive, polished appearance of the community more than Columbia, home of the University of Missouri. So when it came time for Forrest to enroll in college, he chose the University of Kansas.

The younger Allen always said he simply liked Lawrence better than Columbia, but you would think, as an athlete and one who was pretty good at basketball, he had to have been at least a little bit attracted to KU because James Naismith, the father of the game, was also in Lawrence.

The first time Forrest Allen and Naismith met, however, was not in Lawrence but at a March 1905 game in Kansas City's Convention Hall. Forrest was the center for the Kansas City Athletic Club in a game against the Buffalo Germans. It was a three-game series in which Naismith was asked to serve as referee for the final game. The Kansas City team won, based in large part on Allen's free-throw ability.

When the game was over, Naismith asked Forrest Allen to consider playing at the University of Kansas. Unbeknownst to anyone at the time, this day would surely be looked back upon as one of the most pivotal in the history of the game.

Forrest Allen was an athlete of many sports. To pay tuition and other expenses at KU, he began umpiring baseball. Quite the showman as well, one with a deep, powerful voice, he made calls that could be heard loud and clear throughout the ball field, earning him the nickname Foghorn. Later a sportswriter attempting to embody the unique aspects of Foghorn's personality spelled the name "Phog."

Phog Allen played under Naismith's tutelage for just one season, until he was offered a job at nearby Baker University to coach the basketball team. The inventor of basketball responded with his famous pronouncement: "You can't coach basketball. You just play it." This is one of many times that Phog would disagree with his mentor. He believed coaching was essential, and he planned to teach his team better passing and shooting skills while improving their overall physical condition.

While he was coaching at Baker, Phog also coached at nearby Haskell Indian College in Lawrence. It is believed by many that Phog Allen was the first paid college basketball coach in the United States.

In the meantime, Naismith's responsibilities with the ath-letic department and as a professor, along with his theological interests, left little time for coaching basketball, a task he admit-tedly put low on his priority list. Despite their love for Dr. Nai-smith, the fans and administration wanted more.

So James Naismith stepped aside as coach of the game he invented, opening the door for Phog Allen to return in 1907 as coach of basketball and football. He was twenty-two years old.

During those first few years of coaching and in his own rough-and-tumble sports career, Phog learned firsthand about the potential for injuries to upset a game, end a career, or even end a life. Recognizing that he would be a better coach if he could help prevent injuries and treat his players, Phog put his coaching career on hold and entered the Central College of Osteopathy in Kansas City, Missouri.

Two years later, Coach Allen was officially Dr. Allen, and over the years, though others knew him simply as Phog, his play-ers would affectionately call him Doc. He earned an excellent reputation for treating athletes other medical specialists had writ-ten off. Among the bigger names he "cured" were Casey Stengel and Johnny Mize of the New York Yankees.

But Phog wanted to get back into coaching. William Hamilton was doing a great job at KU, so Phog was pleased to receive a job offer in Warrensburg at what today is known as the University of Central Missouri.

The Allens were delighted with the move to Warrensburg. Phog's wife, Bessie, had received a teaching certificate there and Phog had visited the community several times in his coaching career. Three of the five Allen children would be born there.

However, Phog Allen's spirited personality, which was a source of inspiration and affection later in his career, became his undoing at Central Missouri. Although his football, basketball, and baseball teams dominated in conference play, respect from the opposing teams did not accompany those victories.

The Central Missouri team and its coach were officially charged with unsportsmanlike conduct, which included everything from stealing signals and using ineligible players and extensive profanity. Phog Allen was burned in effigy on many campuses and eventually his team was kicked out of the Mid-America Intercollegiate Athletics Association, a ban that lasted two years.

If it hadn't been for this bit of nastiness, the Allens probably would have been content to stay in Warrensburg for the extent of Phog's career. Could Allen Field House have been built in Johnson County, Missouri, instead of Douglas County, Kansas? Would the University of Central Missouri Mules have become as formidable on the court as the Kansas Jayhawks?

Even more unsettling are the ramifications if Phog Allen had accepted a position at Kansas State University in Manhattan! Another job offer came from the Fighting Illini at the University of Illinois, all very real possibilities at the time.

But the hands of fate intervened. The University of Kansas was in need of an athletic director, and even though James Naismith, still on the faculty at KU, recommended another coach, Phog Allen got the job.

That was not the first time, nor would it be the last, that Dr. Naismith and Dr. Allen didn't agree on how to run an athletic department or particularly a basketball program. The first, of course, is that James Naismith didn't believe basketball, as an activity, needed to be coached.

Naismith wasn't crazy about the idea of dribbling. His original Rule #1 was that the ball could be thrown in any direction, but according to Rule #3, a player could not run with the ball. The idea was to pass the ball. No one had ever heard of or thought of dribbling a ball in 1891.

Dribbling was introduced in 1900 and Phog loved it. In fact, when other coaches began to talk of eliminating or reducing the dribble in 1927, Phog's outrage and plan of action not only saved the dribble, but also resulted in the organization of the National Association of Basketball Coaches. Phog Allen was the first president and James Naismith was the honorary president.

Among the more contentious issues between the two that was never resolved during Naismith's lifetime was the height of the goals. Allen absolutely detested those ten-foot-high goals. He fought long and hard to get rid of ten-foot hoops and the congestion that occurred under the goals. He advocated twelve-foot hoops to avoid dunking, minimize fouls, and increase field goals. In fact, he believed so firmly in it that he authorized the construction of twelve-foot goals on the practice floor in the old Robinson gym on KU. The Jayhawks would be prepared.

Naismith never understood Allen's preoccupation with the height of the hoops. He liked the hoops where they were and apparently so did the NCAA rules committee. Today goals in high schools and colleges throughout the United States and around the world remain at ten feet.

But the two men also agreed on a good many things about the game, probably most important, the role and responsibility of physical activity and physical educators. Naismith was concerned especially with the spiritual conditioning of an athlete, and Allen was concerned about academic and social skills, but both believed there was more to life than sports. They called it "the science of developing a boy into a man."

They both agreed that the center tip-off after each score, as Naismith had originally designed the play, gave each team an equal advantage. Allen was on the NCAA rules committee in 1937 when the center jump was eliminated and changed to the current throw-in by the offensive team. As medical professionals, they believed the players needed a few seconds to catch their breath and refocus mentally. Too much nonstop action was stressful not only for players but also for spectators, and created a game that Allen felt came too close to the nonstop rough play of hockey.

As early as a 1910 game between the archrivals Missouri and Kansas, a contest where aggressive play has been a part of the action for more than one hundred years, Naismith was quoted as saying "Oh, my gracious. They are murdering my game."

It's sobering to recognize that both Naismith and Allen, the father of basketball and the father of basketball coaching, feared the influence of money over their game, from gambling and scholarships to alumni and corporate influences.

Although Naismith and Allen were not necessarily close friends, they were respected colleagues. When Allen succeeded in a relentless campaign to get basketball recognized as an Olympic sport, he would not rest until he had implemented a funding campaign for the aging Naismith to attend the games in Berlin and distribute the medals to the athletes. For one week in the winter of 1936, a penny from every gate receipt in college games throughout the country went to a fund to send Naismith to Berlin, followed by a tour of Europe.

Later, the otherwise understated Naismith recalled that watching his game premiere as an Olympic sport was "the happiest moment of my life."

The man who invented basketball rarely missed a game at KU, but neither did he comment about it. In fact, reports say he had few reactions at all as he watched Phog Allen's success as coach of an activity that didn't need coaching. Those who attended the games with him said that Naismith never cheered or applauded. He just watched and went home, and certainly didn't visit Allen's office the next day to relive the game in play-by-play details. Maybe it was simply Naismith's reserved personality or maybe he just didn't care that much.

Naismith died in Lawrence on November 28, 1939, shortly after his seventy-eighth birthday. The entrance to Lawrence Memorial Park Cemetery honors his final resting place with a carved memorial showing him with a basketball under one arm and a stack of textbooks in another.

Just a few months before Naismith's death, the first national college basketball championship tournament had been held in Kansas City, Missouri. This marked the beginning of the national phenomenon now known as March Madness, one of many major developments in the game orchestrated by Phog Allen.

He had long advocated for better facilities for all Kansas athletics. For those who think he was a single-minded proponent of basketball, it's important to remember that he was first successful at raising the funds for football's Memorial Stadium. Although it took more than six years to complete, by 1927, it was considered a palace at the time and has since seen its share of exciting sports moments.

A better facility for basketball was another story. When Naismith was in charge of KU basketball, the "activity" was taught in the basement of Snow Hall. Robinson Gymnasium became the Jayhawk home court in 1907, and then in 1929 the game moved to the three thousand–seat Hoch Auditorium, which was really a performing arts center. Known none too affectionately by all who played there as a "house of horrors"—a moniker that reflected not the Jayhawk forces but the cramped playing space—Hoch contributed to dozens of injuries as players ran and jumped on the concrete floor or slammed into concrete walls.

Of course, any possibility of funding or resources was out of the question until the end of World War II. Even the great Phog Allen couldn't overcome that. When the war ended, somehow rival Kansas State University secured funding for a new field house before KU got it together, totally inflaming Phog Allen's competitive nature.

Finally the Kansas legislature appropriated money in April 1949 and the barn raising on the KU campus began in 1952. The Korean War slowed the construction process, allowing for plenty of time to debate the name of this auspicious new facility. The James Naismith Field House was an obvious choice, and others envisioned the Naismith-Allen Field House. Few other suggestions were ever taken seriously.

At long last, on March 1, 1955, Allen Field House, located on James Naismith Drive, was dedicated on the University of Kansas campus. Fifteen months later, at the mandatory state retirement age of seventy, Phog Allen stepped down as coach of the Kansas Jayhawks. He had coached for forty-eight years, thirty-nine of those at the University of Kansas, where his record was 590 wins and 219 losses.

He died on September 16, 1974, at eighty-eight years old. He and his wife, Bessie, are buried in Oak Hill Cemetery in Lawrence, just across the street from James Naismith's burial site at Lawrence Memorial Park Cemetery.

More than a half century later, people talk of the goose bumps that run up their spine as they enter Allen Field House and gaze upon James Naismith Court. They express a connection to history here that others feel at national parks and designated historic sites. Today's players say they feel the spirit of Phog Allen, the legendary sixth man who has supported each team since the day Phog Allen retired from coaching.

This isn't a reaction by emotionally giddy college kids, but by big names of the game, from Wilt Chamberlain to Roy Williams, and those of all calibers who at some point in their lives have thrown a ball at a hoop. Basketball fans from around the world travel to Lawrence to walk the grounds these legends walked before.

However, had James Naismith not come to Kansas and Phog Allen gone elsewhere, or vice versa, had the two never met or never interacted on the intimate, almost daily basis that they did for almost twenty years, how would the game be played today? If Lambert Will really did contribute a rule or two, should he receive credit in Kansas and beyond? How would Lawrence and all of Kansas look today? And would the Kansas Jayhawks continue, year after year, to reach the pinnacle of the nation's best team in college basketball?

CHAPTER 6

When General George Armstrong Custer Deserted His Post

We've all done stupid things in the name of love. But was George Armstrong Custer's desertion of his post on the Kansas plains to visit his wife an act of love or just one of many impetuous decisions in the young commander's life that foretold his final and most famous act, one that resulted in his death and that of more than 350 American soldiers and American Indians?

An Internet search of the name George Armstrong Custer produces hundreds of thousands of results, many of them in relation to the infamous Battle of the Little Bighorn, often called Custer's Last Stand. For those not familiar with the story, 263 soldiers, including Custer, met their death at the hands of an estimated 1,500 Cheyenne, Arapahoe, and Lakota Sioux warriors on an open plain in southeastern Montana on June 25–26, 1876.

Over the years, the battle and Custer's leadership decisions, along with those of Chief Sitting Bull, have been analyzed, debated, dissected, and reenacted ad nauseam.

However, true scholars of the Little Bighorn begin their study of the battle as far back as December 5, 1839, the date of Custer's birth in Ohio. They include his years at West Point and his accomplishments in the Civil War, and continue by devoting a serious amount of brainpower to Custer's military career in Kansas. Those days in Kansas, covering 1866 to 1871, encompass Custer's first encounter with American Indians, an exploit known lightheartedly as Custer's "mad dash across Kansas," and eventually a court-martial at Fort Leavenworth in 1867.

Critics of Custer's actions often point to his bottom-of-the-class rank at West Point but fail to acknowledge that half of the class were Southerners who disappeared during their senior year to fight for the Confederate cause. Custer supporters believe that a larger class would have improved his class rank. Others point out that Custer was always in trouble at West Point, another argument that maybe he wasn't that smart. But a closer examination shows that most of Custer's demerits were for things like instigating a snowball fight and letting his eyes wander during inspection.

A constant in Custer's life and a considerable influence on his story from a Kansas perspective is his wife, Libbie. An undeniably beautiful and petite woman from an affluent family in Monroe Michigan, Elizabeth Clift Bacon entered Custer's life during a visit to his half-sister's home in October 1861. They married in an elegant ceremony in February 1864.

Author Thom Hatch called her "a model army wife" who endured "the sacrifices and hardships of the Civil War and frontier life without complaint." However, it would be wrong to think of Libbie Custer as a dutiful little housewife simply going where she was told. She was well educated and a talented writer. From her earliest words about the man she called "Autie," letters and personal accounts that have been published extensively, she never expressed doubt for the life she was prepared to lead:

"He is noble, brave and generous and he loves, I believe, with an intensity that few know of or as few ever can love. . . ."

Although much can be debated about the life of George Armstrong Custer, no one may rightfully call into question the mutual adoration and devotion shared by Libbie and Autie Custer.

The two had been married slightly more than two years when in 1866, by an act of Congress, the Seventh Cavalry was formed at Fort Riley, Kansas, and Custer was appointed second in command. Today Fort Riley continues to thrive and is renowned as home of the "Big Red One," the First Infantry Division, the oldest in the US Army. The Custer House, built in 1855, remains intact and is part of a historical tour of the base.

The Custers arrived in central Kansas in early November 1866, along with Eliza, their personal maid, and a young woman named Diana from Monroe, Michigan, who would assist Libbie in decorating and entertaining in her new home and otherwise be an appropriate female companion in Autie's long absences. Autie's brother, Tom, would join them a few months later.

Of their arrival at Fort Riley, Libbie wrote in her book, *Tenting on the Plains,* "I then realized, for the first time, that we had reached a spot where the comforts of life could not be had for love or money."

She also wrote, "The wind blew unceasingly for the five years we were in Kansas," but her observations were not necessarily complaints. She seemed amazed and challenged by the elements and even wrote of sewing lead weights in the hem of her skirts so they would not billow over her head or wrap around Autie's legs during their evening walks.

Custer's job responsibilities required that he oversee a new unit charged with protecting the regional farming settlements, the development of the Union Pacific Railroad, and commerce along the Santa Fe Trail. It was a far-reaching assignment that covered parts of what is today Nebraska, Colorado, Oklahoma, and New Mexico.

Of those first few weeks and months, Libbie's innocence and naïveté were apparent. "Ah! what happy days they were, for at the time I had not the slightest realization of what Indian warfare was, and consequently no dread."

It's generally agreed that the military assigned here faced some of the most difficult conflicts in the period known as the Indian Wars. Military historians of this period would discuss events at Sand Creek, Fort Sedgwick, and the Battle of Washita, and the tragic deaths of Lieutenant Lyman Kidder and his party. There were brutalities on both sides. American Indians and whites who came to the plains either by choice or by military assignment did what was required to survive. Their actions,

George Armstrong Custer

Libbie Custer

although incomprehensible and reprehensible by twenty-first-century standards, were culturally appropriate at the time.

Despite the challenges before them, most of the enlisted men were deeply inexperienced in combat. Those who had fought in the Civil War faced an entirely different enemy on the southern plains. Many of these men developed problems with alcohol and gambling. Desertion became a daily and open occurrence.

In addition, many of the enlisted and even the officers of rank equal to or greater than Custer lacked respect for the man who had become a general at age twenty-three. Despite his exemplary service record during the Civil War, they were jealous of his success, something Custer never failed to brag about. On top of that, his sister and wife had convinced him of the evils of alcohol, so Custer often gave lectures and discipline based on the abuse of alcohol.

But overall Custer was just an exuberant, energetic, and optimistic person. Libbie called him "buoyant" and after a while, that kind of personality gets under some people's skin.

As the day approached that the men would leave for the first major campaign, the realities of Indian warfare had set in for Libbie. The violence between white settlers and Plains Indians had escalated, and tales of the atrocities had reached the protected women of the post. Autie asked that Libbie refrain from tears in his presence. Yet, as distraught with worry as she was, in later years she often commented how privileged she was to be so much nearer the expedition than the families of men who had returned east.

Custer's first serious interaction with the Indians of the Great Plains came in April 1867, when Southern Cheyenne and Sioux were encountered on a regimental march from Fort Harker to Fort Larned under the command of General Winfield Scott Hancock. Custer and the cavalry were dispatched to pursue small parties of fleeing Indians without success. There is a tremendous amount of back-and-forth between historians about the ineptness of General Hancock at this time. Or perhaps it was a period of learning by the US Army about a new enemy and a new battle style. Nonetheless, there was a great deal of frustration in the military ranks as they were outsmarted or outmaneuvered by the enemy.

It was at this time that Custer committed one of his more impetuous and inarguably reckless acts while stationed in Kansas. Right in the midst of it all, Autie took off on his own private buffalo hunt. While riding ahead of his regiment by a mile or two, he spied a lone buffalo and simply decided to follow it and shoot the beast. Perhaps Autie was bored and just needed a break from the stress. Maybe he thought he was back at West Point and felt the need to figuratively throw a snowball at somebody. Who knows? It just doesn't make sense and was extremely dangerous, particularly when the career military officer accidently shot his own horse and became lost, alone and on foot in territory filled with the enemy.

Those under his command came looking for him and everyone eventually arrived safely at Fort Hays. However, Custer complicated the danger of the situation by sending a few troops back to retrieve his saddle from the dead horse—all this in a territory where the enemy openly roamed and easily outnumbered the army.

Waiting for Custer at Fort Hays were a number of letters from Libbie. She expressed her loneliness and boredom without him at Fort Riley. He became depressed and irritable and even more frustrated with the state of affairs. George Custer, the impetuous little boy or the egotistical officer, was not having a good time and he took it out on those around him.

The days and weeks went by, and letters passed between the two. The couple were so eager to be together as much as possible that they often put themselves and others in danger. One situation easily could have resulted in Libbie's death.

In June 1867 the couple had been separated just a few weeks, exchanging letters on a regular basis, when Autie recognized that he would be stationed along the banks of the Platte River for several weeks based on orders given by his superior, General William T. Sherman.

Custer sent a letter asking his wife to travel from Fort Riley to Fort Wallace, where he would have a squadron waiting to accompany her to his outpost in Nebraska. Because of the high number of desertions, it's hard to say exactly how many men were involved, but it's fair to say at least one hundred soldiers, along with their horses, wagons, and support teams, were devoted to this little jaunt.

Well, thank goodness his letter didn't reach Libbie.

The squadron was also to escort a supply train back from Fort Wallace, when in reality, General Sherman had ordered Custer to get supplies from Fort Sedgwick.

Having acquired the needed supplies, but not finding Libbie Custer at the fort, the squadron and wagon train began their return journey to Nebraska when they were attacked by a band of Sioux and Cheyenne. The fight became fairly intense, with casualties on both sides. During this period on the Great Plains, the standing order for all military personnel was, if under attack, to shoot any white woman to prevent her capture by Indians.

Had Libbie made the journey her husband had requested, there is a good chance she would have died violently in remote Kansas rather than nearly sixty years later in the comfort of her New York home.

Although Libbie was safe, the risk to others was not over.

As a result of Custer's not sending a squadron to Fort Sedgwick for supplies, as Sherman had ordered, Lieutenant Lyman Kidder and ten men were sent to find Custer and deliver the orders that had been waiting for him at Fort Sedgwick. Those eleven men instead rode directly into a war party and died a torturous death that would foreshadow the brutality a decade later at the Little Bighorn.

That Custer undermined Sherman's order and made such a major commitment of resources for the primary purpose of spending a few days with his wife has certainly been called into question over the years.

Author Robert Utley sums it well by writing in *Cavalier in Buckskin: George Custer Armstrong and the Western Military Frontier* that "his every major decision for the rest of the operation had more to do with Libbie than with Sherman, Indians, his mission or the welfare of his command."

You would think Custer would have learned to restrain himself, particularly after he led the group that discovered and buried the mutilated bodies of the Kidder party. But when it came to Libbie, Custer's thoughts and actions were myopic to the point of irrational.

He couldn't be satisfied with the fact that, although they were not together, she was indeed safe and out of harm's way at Fort Riley.

Just two weeks later, after several brutal days in the searing Kansas heat and sun, with limited water and rations for both humans and animals, Custer led a bedraggled column back to Fort Wallace. There's much that could be discussed here about how far out of the scope of Sherman's orders Custer had traveled and his orders to shoot deserters at this time, but that detracts from Custer's next act of lunacy.

Despite the desperate physical and mental condition of his troops and no orders other than to rest and recuperate, Custer immediately assembled four officers and seventy-five men and took off to Fort Riley to see Libbie. They covered 150 miles in the scorching summer heat in just fifty-five hours.

At one point, men were sent back a few miles to collect a lost horse, and those men came under attack. Two were killed, but Custer did not slow his pace or allow others the time to recover their bodies.

At Fort Harker, Custer left his troops behind and boarded a train for Fort Riley. Of the moment he stepped unexpectedly into her doorway, Libbie wrote, "With a flood of sunshine that poured in, came a vision far brighter than even the brilliant Kansas sun. There before me, blithe and buoyant, stood my husband. What did earth hold for us greater than what we then had?"

Well, unfortunately, Autie's commanders didn't look at the chain of events through such rose-colored glasses. Within hours of his return to Libbie's arms, Custer received a telegram commanding him to return immediately to Fort Harker, where he was placed under arrest and charged with a number of infractions.

The court-martial took place at Fort Leavenworth in September. The principal charges were leaving command without proper authority and a three-parter that spoke to risk of life, including the deaths of two soldiers, during this mad dash across Kansas.

Six weeks later, Custer was found guilty on all charges and suspended for one year. And although that sounds disastrous to any military career, and certainly criminal in some cases, a court-martial in 1867 was not the serious event that it is today.

Many followers of the Custer legacy inaccurately assume that he was stripped of his rank at this time. Indeed, he was promoted to general during the Civil War, but after the war, the military downsized and many officers lost their rank. At one point Custer was demoted as low as captain, through no fault of his own. When he was appointed to the Seventh Cavalry, he returned as a lieutenant colonel, the rank he maintained despite the court-martial. However, as complicated as it appears, because Custer had once ranked as a general, it was common courtesy and appropriate to be called general. It becomes extremely confusing when those with what appears to be a lower rank have a higher command.

After the court-martial, Autie and Libbie lost their officer's housing at Fort Leavenworth. General Philip Sheridan, commander of the fort, was one of many at the time who felt Hancock and others had reacted harshly and vindictively in their charges. Therefore, he took an extended leave and offered the Custers use of his quarters at 611 Scott. The building still stands at Fort Leavenworth today.

The Custers, however, did not remain in disgrace. Instead, they were welcomed guests at many homes and entertained frequently at 611 Scott. They enjoyed the support and friendship of many of the nearly one thousand military families housed at Fort Leavenworth at the time.

In June 1868 the Custers returned to the comforts of Monroe, Michigan, for the remainder of Autie's suspension. Then in

September 1868 he received a telegram from General Sheridan asking that he return to duty with the Seventh Cavalry as soon as possible. Things had been going very badly indeed for the army, and it became clear that Custer's aggressive style and tenacity would turn the tide.

Custer returned to Kansas as a victor, confident in the support of his superiors and welcomed by enlisted men eager for his acumen and leadership in the matters at hand. He returned to field command at Fort Dodge, and, of course, Libbie accompanied him.

There were a number of campaigns that took the Seventh Cavalry throughout Kansas, Oklahoma, and Texas for the better part of two years. Custer's reputation and the tranquility of their marriage was certainly challenged at this time, as fairly well-documented accusations revealed an intimate and long-term relationship between the general and a Cheyenne woman captured at the Battle of Washita. The woman had a baby that Cheyenne legend says was Custer's child.

Other stories suggest Libbie engaged in inappropriate conduct at Fort Leavenworth, but perhaps those were rumors started by those who testified against Custer at his court-martial. Who knows?

But in the end, under Custer's leadership, the central and southern Plains Indians were eventually overpowered and their culture nearly eradicated from the American landscape. The next battlefront lay in the northern plains.

In March 1871 the Custers left Fort Leavenworth and Kansas for the last time. Campaigns through the Yellowstone Basin and the Black Hills ensued, and in November 1873 they arrived at what would become their final post at Fort Abraham Lincoln, North Dakota. At the time of his death in June 1876, Autie and Libbie Custer had been married twelve years and four months.

Years later, of their days in Kansas Libbie wrote fondly of many experiences but remembered most distinctly the day on which her husband arrived unexpectedly at Fort Riley, the day that resulted in his court-martial. "There was in that summer of 1867 one long, perfect day. It was mine, and—blessed be our memory, which preserves to us the joys as well as the sadness of life—it is still mine, for time and for eternity."

CHAPTER 7

Dwight David Eisenhower

W ho was it that stole a fortune from the Eisenhower family, and where did they disappear to with all that money? How did these circumstances that impoverished the Eisenhower family change the man who would lead the D-Day invasion and become the thirty-fourth president of the United States?

A number of legendary figures who made a lasting impact on the Old West and a developing nation lived in or passed through Kansas. But without question, no one had a greater impact on the freedom of the entire world than a little boy, born in Denison, Texas, who moved to Abilene, Kansas, in 1892 when he was still a toddler in his mother's arms.

His name, registered in the family Bible on October 14, 1890, was David Dwight Eisenhower, named after his father, David. But everyone called him Dwight, and soon he began signing his name as Dwight David, the third of what would be six sons born to David and Ida Eisenhower.

But it was what happened to David and Ida just two years before their third son's birth that altered the course of Dwight's life perhaps more than any other event, and, as such, could have changed the path of global freedom in the twentieth century and beyond.

In the hundreds of books and scholarly articles on the life of Dwight David Eisenhower, little has been written about this time in the little town of Hope, Kansas, shortly after the future president's parents married. But the devastation on the Eisenhower family was so drastic that it set into motion a course of events that probably contributed more to the strength, stamina, and direction of this world leader than anything else that occurred in his brilliantly successful and far-reaching life.

David Eisenhower, the president's father, was fourteen when his family moved to Abilene from Pennsylvania, part of a large congregation of River Brethren church members. There were four children in the family of Jacob and Rebecca Eisenhower: David, Amanda, Ira, and Abraham. Unlike many who came to Kansas at that time, the Eisenhowers were not penniless. They had been well established for several generations in this country and the farm and large home in Pennsylvania sold for a healthy price.

Jacob Eisenhower was both a farmer and a River Brethren minister, so the house they built on their 160-acre farm served as both a family home and a meeting place for the congregation. As the four children became old enough to marry and leave home,

Jacob gave each of them 160 acres and $2,000 as wedding gifts. That's about $1 million in modern terms, give or take a few hundred dollars. Not a bad way to start off married life.

However, David Eisenhower was not interested in farming. His talent and interests were more mechanical in nature. He excelled in dissecting and repairing machinery and wanted to go to college to learn more in this field, maybe even become an engineer.

It was while he was attending the now-defunct Lane College in Lecompton, Kansas, that David Eisenhower met and fell in love with Ida Elizabeth Stover, a young woman with a bright mind, a beautiful smile, and a small inheritance of her own. They were married on September 23, 1885.

Prior to their wedding, David became acquainted with Milton Good, a young man about his age who worked at a clothing store in Abilene. The two formed a partnership and opened a general store in the community of Hope, about twenty miles south of Abilene. Milton had the retail experience and David had the capital. By mortgaging his 160 acres, David was able to contribute $4,000 to the enterprise. Milton Good was recently married as well and the two couples lived in adjoining apartments above the store they worked in.

The first two years were great. The Goods and the Eisenhowers were happy and well liked in the community and the store was always busy. David and Ida gave birth to their first son, Arthur. David trusted his partner to take care of the bookkeeping until the summer of 1888, when it became apparent that too many townspeople had been extended too much credit and were not paying their bills. To pay their creditors and to keep the store afloat, David relied on Ida's inheritance.

By this time, however, relations between Milton Good and David Eisenhower were strained. Perhaps they had a big fight or perhaps the strain and tension of it all became too much, but sometime in the fall of 1888, without telling anyone, Milton Good and his wife left Hope, never to return or be heard from again.

Within days, David Eisenhower discovered the horrible truth. Not only had his partner skipped town, but neither had he paid any of the bills he said had been paid, and David and Ida were left holding the bag for several thousand dollars of debt.

They liquidated all of their assets, except Ida's ebony piano, and David sought work elsewhere. He found it with a railroad in Denison, Texas, and he left immediately. Ida was very much pregnant with their second child, Edgar, and didn't join her husband until after the baby was born.

The couple struggled desperately in Denison, surviving on next to nothing while they sent the little money they had to creditors. The only good thing that happened to them while in Texas was the birth of their third son, the future president of the United States, on October 14, 1890.

There was little to celebrate with this baby, however, just another mouth to feed as they attempted to repair their finances.

Milton, David, Dwight, Ida, Earl, and the family dog, Flip, at their home in Abilene in 1910.

David and Ida returned to Kansas less than two years after they had left, two toddlers in tow and a soon-to-be five-star general traveling in his mother's arms.

Soon there were six Eisenhower boys growing up in a little white frame house at 201 Southeast Fourth, on the south side of the tracks. The house still stands with its original furnishings as a part of the Eisenhower Presidential Museum and Library complex in Abilene. Looking at it today, it's remarkable that nine people, a number that included Grandfather Jacob for several years, could find space for themselves within the confines of the tiny home of little more than eight hundred square feet. Equally remarkable is that the little house did not simply implode from the energy of six rambunctious boys.

Despite the wealth that had once been a part of the larger Eisenhower family, the household in which Dwight was raised was not one of affluence. Grandfather Jacob's financial condition had diminished significantly when the bank he had invested in failed. David had been given his inheritance and it had not turned out well. David's only option was to accept a job as a mechanic at the Belle Springs Creamery. It was a good job and offered a steady, albeit small income for the family.

Therefore, everyone in the Eisenhower family needed to work and help earn money for the family at the earliest possible age. The boys were primarily responsible for a huge garden and orchard, selling excess fruits and vegetables around town. Of course, on a daily basis there were cows to be milked and other livestock to be cared for, eggs to be collected and sold from the family chicken coop, firewood to be split, and so on and on.

The boys also cooked, washed dishes, did laundry, and cleaned house on a strict but fair schedule their mother devised. Their responsibilities rotated weekly so that each boy would learn the responsibilities of maintaining a household yet would not become bored with one chore.

Such a plan worked out pretty well, except for the weeks that Dwight was responsible for being the first up to stir the fire and warm the house. The future West Point cadet apparently was not a fan of early reveille, and years later as adults the boys would complain that Dwight never fulfilled those duties to the best of his abilities.

Like so many others reared in that time period and in similar situations, the boys were not aware that they were poor until others pointed it out to them. That, of course, happened first at school and later as the boys, with their wagon filled with fruits and vegetables, knocked on the doors of their wealthier neighbors.

Of course, the boys wore hand-me-down clothing that was patched and worn, sometimes ill-fitting, and certainly not stylish. The family could not afford shoes for the boys, so they wore their mother's old button-top shoes, a little fashion faux pas not lost on the children from more prosperous families with whom the Eisenhower boys attended school.

In almost every examination of Dwight Eisenhower's childhood, story after story is told of the humiliation and disgrace the boys felt as they drove a buggy or pulled their wagon through town, knocking at the back doors in Abilene's wealthy neighborhoods north of the tracks. Over the years, each of the boys, from oldest to youngest, spoke of their extreme discomfort and emotional pain.

"They'd make us feel like beggars," Edgar later told Eisenhower biographer Kenneth S. Davis. The housewives or their maids frequently criticized the quality of the produce and demanded prices even lower than the very few pennies the Eisenhower children were asking for their hard labors.

As they grew older and began to notice the young women of Abilene, the Eisenhower boys became painfully aware that some girls were just off limits to the poor kids from the south side of the tracks. In interviews and his personal writings later in life, Dwight Eisenhower downplayed this class distinction, but a number of his friends and his brothers politely but firmly disagreed with the commander in chief.

In June 1945, when the supreme commander of the Allied Expeditionary Forces returned to Abilene for the first time since liberating Europe, the homecoming parade passed directly in front of the homes of many of the families that had looked down upon the little boy who had sold produce at their back doors.

On June 4, 1952, when the five-star general announced his candidacy for president of the United States from the Plaza Theatre in Abilene, it's likely that the audience included many of those girls who wouldn't give Dwight Eisenhower the time of day forty years earlier.

However, as a result of Ida's teachings and the religious environment in which the boys were raised, they never learned to hate these people who caused them such pain. With the exception of Adolf Hitler, whom the military commander admits that he did truly hate, Dwight Eisenhower said later that he felt only a need to overcome the meanness that caused people to be so hurtful to those around them.

He certainly could have used his power and position later in life to return the rudeness he endured. It would have been tempting to use the resources at his disposal, such as the Internal Revenue Service, to find the whereabouts of Milton Good who had done such emotional and financial harm to his family, but Dwight Eisenhower chose the higher road.

In his memoir *At Ease: Stories I Tell to Friends,* the president tells of a time in his youth when he lost his temper for not being allowed to go trick-or-treating with Arthur and Edgar. Young Dwight took out his frustrations by beating his fists into an apple tree and his father, in turn, taught him a lesson with a hickory switch. Later, as Ida bandaged her son's injured hands and soothed his injured spirit, she quoted from the Bible: "He that conquereth his own soul is greater than he who taketh a city," a foretelling scripture lesson for the man who, forty years later, would lead others in storming the beaches of Normandy.

But her lesson was one that echoed throughout the lifetime of this future world leader—that learning to control one's temper and not allowing hatred to enter one's soul is a valued and necessary skill for anyone hoping to live a peaceful, productive, and happy life. David and Ida were living examples of that lesson for their sons. They could have become angry and bitter at the man who stole from them, and raised their children in a home filled with such harmful emotions, but they, too, chose the higher road.

A huge turning point in the lives of all of the Eisenhower family came in 1908. The little house on Southeast Fourth Street got indoor plumbing. An addition to the house was built that included a bathroom and a downstairs bedroom for the parents.

The six boys spread out over three very small bedrooms upstairs, and life was good.

Another turning point that certainly would have altered or ended the life of Dwight Eisenhower happened when he was about fourteen. While running with some friends, he somehow fell, ripping a hole in a new pair of pants and scraping up his knee pretty good—something that had happened a thousand times already. But the next day, the leg became infected and for the next two weeks, Dwight was in and out of consciousness with a raging fever and infection racing through his body.

Carbolic acid, which was used as an antiseptic at that time, was regularly applied around the boy's waist and according to memories of John Eisenhower, "Dad claimed that when they put that carbolic acid around his waist, you could hear him yell in the next county."

Not one but two doctors checked on his condition several times a day and Dwight overheard them talking about amputating the leg. The president later wrote, "At that time my ambitions were directed toward excellence in sports, particularly baseball and football. I could not imagine an existence in which I was not playing one or both."

So Edgar, who was always Dwight's ally in tough times, promised his younger brother that he would do everything in his might to stop an amputation. For days he slept on the floor at the door to the little downstairs room where Dwight lay unconsciousness and in pain. Anyone who came in the room had to get past Edgar first.

The president later complained that the story had been overblown and written out of context so many times that he didn't even recognize it, but John Eisenhower remembered that the story was often retold at family get-togethers.

"They took great pride in Ed's role, standing in the door and declaring that Dwight would rather die than lose his leg," John said. "It seems to fit in with their military mindset. They were a real bunch of roughnecks."

However, the family surely recognized the dramatic alteration that would have occurred in Dwight's life and, in turn, the course of world events had he lost his leg to that illness. He beat the infection, but it left him so weakened that he had to repeat a year of high school, thus delaying his graduation and later his application to the military academies.

As high school graduation neared for all of the Eisenhower boys, the ability of their parents to offer anything more than their best wishes for a college education was out of the question. David and Ida did encourage their boys and support their goals with all of their might, but they didn't have a penny to contribute to the cause.

Arthur took additional classes in bookkeeping and office work and headed to Kansas City, where he eventually became a leader in the city's banking community. Edgar also knew exactly what he wanted to do. He went to law school at the

University of Michigan. The plan was that Dwight would work for a year after high school and help pay for Edgar's education, then Edgar would take a year off and reciprocate for his younger brother.

However, in the summer of 1910, a year after Dwight had graduated from high school, a young man named Everett Hazlett moved back to Abilene, and the two became fast friends. Dwight, who by this time everyone was calling Ike despite Ida's disapproval, was fascinated by Hazlett's plan to attend the US Naval Academy in Annapolis, Maryland. He had never heard of the military academies and was immediately intrigued by the fact that, if accepted, his education would be provided free of charge.

Of course, he was also intrigued by the physical and academic challenges of the academies. Ida Eisenhower, a pacifist who had witnessed firsthand the horrors of the Civil War from her birthplace in Virginia, did not share her son's enthusiasm.

Dwight's first choice was the Naval Academy with his friend Hazlett, but as it turned out, he was just a few months too old to be accepted, in part because of his delayed high school graduation. West Point was Eisenhower's second choice, one he never regretted.

In a letter to his friend years later, Eisenhower entirely credited his friend "Swede" Hazlett for launching him on his way: "As you well know, it was only through you that I ever heard of the Government Academies. To the fact that you were well acquainted with the methods of entering the Academies and my good fortune that you were my friend, I owe a lifetime of real enjoyment and interesting work."

Of course, the rest is taught in history classes not only throughout the United States, but also around the world. Any US president is certainly a world leader, but Dwight Eisenhower had established his place in world history long before he served two terms in the White House.

Dwight Eisenhower's last visit to Abilene was on November 30, 1967. He and his wife, Mamie, visited the Eisenhower center, including the chapel, and his parents' graves before having lunch with friends at Lena's Restaurant. The restaurant still stands in Abilene today and operates under the name Mr. K's Farmhouse.

He returned permanently on April 2, 1969, five days after he died at Walter Reed Army Hospital in Washington, D.C. Little Dwight Eisenhower, the scrapper who sold vegetables to snooty neighbors and played baseball in empty lots throughout Abilene, was laid to rest in a regular army casket in the soil of Kansas that was a part of every fiber of his being.

But a question about this little Kansas farm boy's rise to leadership and power that has rarely been pondered comes back to that general store in Hope and the theft committed by Milton Good. If David and Ida Eisenhower had not lost all of their money, and David his self-pride and motivation, the six boys surely would have been raised in a much more affluent environment. David's brothers and sister did very well for themselves with the financial gifts from their father.

So had David Eisenhower been able to fund his sons' college educations, would Dwight have left Abilene, probably joining Edgar at the University of Michigan, by the time Swede Hazlett came back to their hometown? If not, Dwight certainly wouldn't have needed a free education, so perhaps the military academies would have had less of an appeal for him and he wouldn't even have applied. Then, who would have led the invasion and liberation of Europe?

And out there somewhere is Milton Good, David's old business partner, who made away with the Eisenhower family fortune.

CHAPTER 8

Children: Free to a Good Home in Kansas

W ho? What? Where? When? Why? These questions, known as the five Ws, are the basics taught in any Journalism 101 class anywhere around the world. They are the foundation of good reporting, but for more than 7,500 children who called Kansas home, the answers to these five questions haunted them every day throughout their lives.

The image in the minds of most individuals as they visualize the influx of settlers into Kansas territory in the late nineteenth and early twentieth centuries probably resembles something along the lines of the opening forty-five seconds of the 1970s television series *Little House on the Prairie.* Although the TV show was set in Minnesota, the image remains of a smiling, happy, eager family traveling by covered wagon to a world of promise and fulfillment.

However, there was a distinct population of Kansans who arrived by train, alone, frightened to tears, and often without any hope that life would ever provide any degree of love or stability. These were children from New York City who had been abandoned, orphaned, or abused. They had no one to care for them and nowhere else to go, so they were shipped west by train to see where their fates would lead.

For some of the children, their train trip west was the answer to their prayers and to the prayers of so many others. For some children, unfortunately, the dream of a happy family waiting at the end of the line turned into a nightmare.

In many cases, youngsters were placed with or adopted into loving families, and then, of course, other times not. Many times the farm families simply needed more children to work the land and help with household chores. The children were considered an investment, like horses or mules, or worse, free labor like the slaves.

Of these children who came to Kansas, a little girl named Alice would eventually become a child psychologist to help other disenfranchised children. A little boy named John would be decorated for service in the Army Medical Corps during World War II. Another boy, who called himself Kansas Charley, would be hanged for double murder by the age of seventeen.

And a woman named Anna Laura Hill did her best to see that these children of Kansas were cared for in the new homes that fate had provided them, and helped to answer their heartbreaking pleas to understand who they were and from where they had come. Most of all, the children wanted to know why.

Although the circumstances were indeed grim, those responsible for sending trainloads of children into the hands of strangers in Kansas and beyond were doing the best possible for those children considering the resources available at the time.

A group of orphaned boys ready to depart New York.

The story for most of them started in the 1850s in the tenement slums of New York, where disease and overall poor living conditions encountered by immigrants often left children without parents to care for them, thus roaming the streets of New York as beggars, thieves, and prostitutes. They received no education and their deplorable day-to-day existence contributed to the overall miserable conditions of the slums.

As a matter of survival, many of the homeless young boys formed into violent and powerful street gangs as portrayed in the 2002 movie *Gangs of New York,* starring Leonardo DiCaprio, Liam Neeson, and Daniel Day-Lewis. The movie is considered authentic to the conditions in parts of New York around 1850.

There were a few orphanages operated by churches and other charitable organizations, but they were overflowing and had limited resources to meet the ever-present and growing demand of homeless and orphaned children in the city. Similar conditions were present in other cities along the East Coast, but New York at that time, as today, had the largest population of immigrants and therefore the most pressing problems. Some estimates put the number at more than thirty thousand homeless, abandoned children in New York in 1850.

In 1853 a number of ministers and other social reformers led by Charles Loring Brace formed the Children's Aid Society based on the belief that children would develop into self-reliant, productive members of society only when they were raised in a family environment, learned the value of hard work, and received a proper education. The effort by Brace and the Children's Aid Society was the first of its kind in the United States. This was the precursor to programs today, such as the Division of Family Services, foster care, and other state and federal programs charged with the welfare of those under the age of eighteen.

The Children's Aid Society started with the orphanages but also took its mission into the streets to find homeless, abandoned children. The first step was to verify if the children had any living relatives willing and able to care for them, an effort made more difficult by language barriers and children so young that they had no memory of the parents who had brought them into the world. The hope is that the Children's Aid Society was successful at this level, but under such desperate conditions and limited record keeping, who knows whether despite all good intentions a few children might have been permanently separated from their parents.

Indeed, one little girl named Georgianna who came to Kansas was separated from a loving father who had been told by orphanage workers that she was dead. Later it was discovered that they had been bribed to tell this lie. Two little boys who also came to Kansas had a father who loved them but could not care for them after their mother died. He promised to connect with them later, but why this never happened, the boys never knew.

Charles Loring Brace and his colleagues believed these children would thrive by living with and working for "morally upright farm families." So the youngsters who were deemed healthy and free of disease were cleaned up and shipped west by train in the company of women and lawyers employed by the Children's Aid Society. During a seventy-five-year period, from 1854 to 1929, more than three hundred thousand children, some as young as two years old, left New York by train and were placed in homes in forty-five states, as well as Canada and Mexico.

Prior to the train's arrival in a community, newspaper advertisements would announce the coming of the train and the details of the forthcoming adoption event. Adoption was not always what happened and the event had striking similarities to a slave auction. Children were lined up on a stage or platform to be inspected by the public.

The audience was frequently filled with curiosity seekers, as well as families hoping to adopt children and farmers hoping to acquire an additional young laborer. Other than the fact that in its early days, the Children's Aid Society provided services only to white children, the event was quite similar to a slave auction, and certainly as demeaning to the children as it had been to slaves.

Later in her life Georgianna Frentz, who was placed with a family in Marion, wrote of the experience, saying, "It was very degrading and humiliating and I felt as if I was on the slave block."

Trains went from town to town to town placing these children on display. And despite the degradation the children surely felt, imagine the discouragement and lethal damage to their feelings of self-worth when, not selected by any of these complete strangers, they were herded back onto the train only to be forced through the ordeal again in the next town down the line.

The Opera House in McPherson was one of the nicer settings for adoption events. The Beloit Opera House also hosted them. Most were held in churches, but some were held on platforms in town squares, just like a slave auction. Independence, Chanute, Fredonia, Cherryvale, and Yates Center all hosted multiple adoption events over the years. Almost fifty other towns saw the orphan train arrive at least once in its seventy-five-year history.

John Lukes was not yet three years old when the orphan train arrived in Ottawa in 1915. Just a few weeks after he was born in June 1912, he had been given to the New York Nursery and Child's Hospital. There is no record of his parents and no reason as to why he was given away.

John was too young to have any memory of the discomfort or humiliation of the adoption event. He was fortunate for another reason: He was one of four children eventually adopted into the loving home of Charles and Edna Jacobus. Charles Jacobus had been the superintendent of the Ottawa schools and also operated a little gift shop with his wife. They encouraged John's natural curiosity and independent nature. In 1934 John Lukes, who was now legally Johnny Jacobus, graduated with a double major in science and math from Ottawa University. He served in the Army Medical Corps during World War II and was in the Philippines during the battle of Leyte Gulf.

John Jacobus eventually married, raised a daughter of his own, and lived a happy, productive life for over eighty-five years.

The story of little Georgianna Frentz Dawson was not so happy. She was born out of wedlock on October 28, 1899, and her grandmother Mary Anna was a Vanderbilt, one of the aristocratic families of nineteenth- and twentieth-century America. Georgianna's mother died of appendicitis, and Georgianna was sent to live with her aunt and uncle, and later to an orphanage. Georgianna's biological father later came looking for her, but the orphanage had received a significant donation from the mother's family to ensure that if anyone came asking about little Georgianna, he or she would be told that she had died and was buried in an unmarked grave.

Georgianna was twelve years old when she rode the orphan train into Kansas and was placed with a family near Marion, a little community just east of McPherson when the adoption event was held. She did well at school and worked hard, but when Anna Laura Hill, the Children's Aid Society placement worker, came to check on her about the time she turned fourteen,

Georgianna said that if she wasn't moved, she would run away from the home she was in. What had happened to the otherwise docile and obedient little Georgianna for her to make this threat?

Anna Hill quickly placed Georgianna with a single, elderly woman more than 150 miles away near Ford, Kansas, where she was given music lessons and taught to cook and sew. Georgianna met and married a local boy named Elmer Dawson, and together they farmed and raised four happy children. Georgianna died at age eighty-two in Dodge City.

Like Georgianna's, James and Charles Hill's mother died at a young age. Their father knew he could not earn a living and properly care for the boys, ages four and two, respectively, so he placed them temporarily with the Five Points House of Industry. The charitable facility was not quite an orphanage but a place where more than four hundred children in similar situations were cared for without charge. Mr. Hill apparently had every intention of reuniting with his children, but why that never happened, no one really knows.

Eventually little James and Charles were on an orphan train headed to Beloit, Kansas. The November 1909 adoption event was the first of its kind in the north central part of the state and the curious of the community turned out in droves. Sixteen children were lined up in chairs on the stage of the Beloit Opera House. The young Hill brothers understood so very little about what was going on around them and clung to each other, as well as to the hope that they would stay together. So many other siblings on the orphan train were separated, never seeing each other again.

In the audience that day were Mr. and Mrs. Lon Seaman, who, unable to have children of their own, had come hoping to take home a little girl. Instead, they were captivated by the charming little boys and their need to stay together. Later the Seamans would separately take in three girls from the orphan train, but on November 19, 1909, James and Charles Hill rode away in a wagon in the care of Mr. and Mrs. Seaman.

The boys did well in school and excelled in sports. They worked hard on the farm and, by all accounts, all of the children placed in Mr. and Mrs. Seaman's home were loved and well cared for. Although the Seamans never legally adopted the children, the boys and girls used the Seaman name when registering for school. It was not unusual at that time for other children to tease or bully those who were foster or adopted children—one of the many emotional challenges these orphan-train children had to overcome in their very young lives.

At some point in their childhood in Beloit, a message came to the Seaman home that a mysterious and large crate had come from New York addressed to the boys and was waiting at the Beloit post office. Mr. Seaman went in to Beloit to pick it up, but the boys never saw it and had no idea who had sent it or what was inside. The boys always believed their biological father had passed away in New York and someone had shipped some of his possessions to the little boys, whom he had left only with a promise that someday he would return for them. Had the crate contained answers to what had happened to their father? And why had Mr. Seaman, who had been so good to all the children in his home, decided not to share the contents with the boys?

Throughout their childhood, Anna Laura Hill, the case-worker with the Children's Aid Society, made regular visits to the Seaman farm to check on the condition of all the foster children there. When James graduated from high school in 1924, Anna's visit was accompanied by the good news that someone had provided funds for him to attend college. Although James had ideas about who it might have been, it was odd that the benefactor had provided for James, but not for his younger brother, Charles. That question has never been answered.

James Hill attended college and worked for more than thirty years with the Missouri Pacific Railroad. He married Isabelle Irene Wertz and together they had eight children. He lived a productive and happy life in Kansas for nearly ninety years.

His brother, Charles, served in the army during World War II and was injured while stationed in the Aleutian Islands off the coast of Alaska. The brothers never saw each other after about 1940 and communicated only irregularly. After his military service, Charles opened an agate mining company in northern Arizona. He loved to hunt and won a number of awards for his photography of mountain lions. Charles died in Arizona, where his ashes were scattered, exactly ninety years after arriving in Beloit.

Then there's the story of the Miller children. They were three boys and a little girl born to German immigrants in the 1870s. The mother died in childbirth and the father, overworked, broke, and despondent in caring for four children, committed suicide in 1881. After a few years in an orphanage, the little girl was placed as a domestic in upstate New York and brothers Fred and Willie went via the orphan train to a farm family near Leonardville, Kansas, a rural community just north of Manhattan.

However, Charley Miller had a problem that made life incredibly difficult for a young boy. He was a bed wetter, a condition that resulted in serious discipline and humiliation at the orphanage. When Charley was twelve, doctors thought they could cure him by performing a circumcision, certainly a very painful operation considering his age and the medical facilities of the time.

Charley was never cured of his bed-wetting, but eventually was sent on an orphan train toward Minnesota. The family there often whipped Charley and didn't allow him to go to school very often. After two years of such abuse, Charley was sent to a family in Randolph, Kansas, just a few miles from brothers Fred and Willie in Leonardville. Despite the improved conditions, the stability of the Miller boys all being in such close proximity, and their ability to see each other, Charley didn't do well there either.

He ran away, riding the rails from here to there, stealing and picking up enough work to eat and survive. He began calling himself Kansas Charley. When he was sixteen years old and in Hillsdale, Wyoming, Charley murdered two boys sharing a boxcar with him. He later confessed and turned himself in to the sheriff in Manhattan, Kansas. A Wyoming jury convicted him of double murder and in April 1892, Kansas Charley was hanged for his crimes, six months before his eighteenth birthday.

The remaining Miller siblings lived out reasonably productive lives, causing very little heartache or trouble in the communities where they were raised. So the questions remain: Why was Charley not as successful in the orphan train experience? Was it his bed-wetting that set the stage for a lifetime of difficulty? Was it the beatings he received from his Minnesota family? Or was it the overall lack of care available to a very needy young boy who might have developed into a responsible adult had he not become an orphan at such an early age?

The circumstances were indeed extraordinary for these children, and it's remarkable that more did not turn to violence as an outlet for their fears, confusion, and frustrations. Some were able to use their painful experiences to improve the lives of other children.

Nine-year-old Alice Bullis Ayler was responsible for three younger brothers and living in a tent in the Catskill Mountains of New York when they were all turned over to the Children's Aid Society. In 1929 they were on one of the last orphan trains to Kansas. The boys were adopted by a family near Arkansas City and Alice was placed in several unhappy homes around Marion. As an adult, Alice married, raised an adopted child of her own, and became a child psychologist in the Oklahoma City public schools. Later she wrote, "Some people are bitter about the trains but not me. Even though there were some hard times, it probably saved my life."

Throughout the children's lives, Anna Laura Hill made regular visits to check on them. A native of Pennsylvania, Anna was twenty-five years old when she began working with the Children's Aid Society. She accompanied children on train trips throughout North America and was assigned specifically to Kansas from 1909 to 1925. The children received Christmas and birthday greetings from Anna; when she died, her files were filled with graduation and marriage announcements from hundreds of the children she had helped receive a new life.

Although an orphan train never stopped at the depot in Concordia, Kansas, today the community is home to the National Orphan Train Museum and Research Library. Throughout the year, orphan-train children and their descendants come to Concordia to better understand this part of their lives and this challenging time in American society. Above all, they come in search of the answers to the very same questions: Who? Why? And what if?

CHAPTER 9

Carry A. Nation in Kansas

Was she really the crazed, hatchet-wielding, Bible-thumping wild woman who destroyed saloons throughout the Midwest or was she simply a brokenhearted woman, kind and loving to children, who simply wanted to be heard? And who was it that knocked on her hotel room door in the middle of the night in Hope, Kansas?

The twenty-first century's late-night comedians, from David Letterman and Jay Leno to Jon Stewart and Stephen Colbert, would salivate for a modern character like Carry Nation. A year's worth of antics from Hollywood's most unbalanced celebrities and Washington's most flamboyant politicians would appear calm and ordinary in comparison to one afternoon of Carry Nation's saloon-smashing street brawls in communities throughout Kansas.

From the beginning of time, humanity has been populated with an intriguing number of eccentric characters, and certainly the population of Kansas has had its fair share over the years.

Few, however, can hold a candle to Carry Nation. Her neighbors in Medicine Lodge became accustomed to Carry on her knees in front of saloons singing hymns and praying aloud at the top of her lungs. The sight of her tussling with town sheriff's deputies while she straddled a barrel of whiskey in the middle of Main Street certainly drew an audience, but for many, it was just another day in Carry Nation–land. But many cynical saloon keepers in Kansas felt ice water run through their veins when they saw Mother Nation's massive figure in their doorway and heard her legendary greeting, "Good morning, destroyer of men's souls."

But what led Carry to such bizarre and drastic actions? Was she just another religious zealot going off the deep end behind a cause? Or was it something more that began burning in Carry's abundant spirit early in her difficult childhood? Perhaps it was something beyond her control, a mental illness that certainly presented itself in Carry's mother, an illness that took a devastating emotional toll on an otherwise delicate and sensitive little girl?

On a large farm in southeastern Kentucky, the Moore family was fairly affluent for the region and time period. They owned a number of slaves and it was from the time she spent living in the slave quarters that Carrie, born in November 1846, received many of her first teachings in religion and faith. She witnessed those around her clap their hands and loudly express their joy in the Lord during worship services, and Carrie envied their emotional freedom.

As the eldest of four children, Carrie adored and was adored by her father, George, but her mother, Mary, was another story. Her unusual behaviors and mood swings today would most certainly result in treatment for what likely was either schizophrenia, bipolar disorder, or any number of similar conditions. She had delusions of grandeur in which she was the queen of England and carried the role so far as to own a gilded carriage and to have her slaves dress in finery reflective of royal carriage drivers. As the carriage traveled through the countryside, they announced the "queen's" presence by blowing a trumpet.

Mary dressed and decorated elegantly, hosted lavish parties, and celebrated the finer things in life. Years later Carrie would wear only very dark, very simple clothing and rid her home of anything but the most basic furnishings. She voiced great contempt for those with extravagant clothing and home furnishings.

Mary went through dark periods where she never left her room. Other times she left her home for long periods, thus leaving the slaves to provide for all of Carrie's needs. At a very young age, Mary would banish Carrie from their home and tell her to sleep and eat with the slaves. Even on her good days, Mary rarely offered her daughter any amount of physical affection.

As the Civil War approached, George Moore decided it would be prudent to move farther from the heart of the trouble to an area just south of Kansas City where other relatives had settled. During their journey, they passed through many areas already devastated by the war, coming upon the Pea Ridge

Carry Amelia Nation

Battlefield in northwest Arkansas just hours after the conclusion of the violent three days that took the lives of more than one thousand men. The vision of the human carnage stayed with Carrie for years.

The family survived the atrocities of war in Missouri and, like everyone else, began to rebuild their lives. As the head of the local school board, Carrie's father, George, offered temporary housing to a newly hired teacher, Dr. Charles Gloyd, a medical doctor from Ohio who hoped to establish a practice nearby.

By now Carrie was nineteen, and although not beautiful, certainly becoming with dark hair, intense eyes, and a tall, slender frame. Dr. Gloyd took a fancy to Carrie, despite her parents' warning that he had a drinking problem. Ignoring her parents' advice, four days before her twenty-first birthday, Carrie Moore became Mrs. Charles Gloyd. The good doctor arrived at the wedding falling-down drunk and slurring his vows. Carrie cried during the long buggy ride to their new home in Holden, Missouri.

Within a week, Gloyd was staying out late, coming home drunk, smoking nonstop, and almost but not entirely ignoring Carrie. She was soon pregnant. Six months after their daughter Charlien was born, Charles Gloyd, the love of Carrie's life, died from alcohol-related illnesses. They had been married sixteen months. Carrie turned to her Bible for comfort and direction.

This next act became typical of Carrie's extensive compassion for others, which has been overshadowed in tales of her radical temperance efforts. Concerned for the overall welfare of Gloyd's mother, Carrie invited her to move with Carrie and the baby to Warrensburg, where Carrie received a teaching certificate from what is now the University of Central Missouri.

This was a major step for Carrie's independence. The next four years, as she taught elementary school, were among the happiest of her life. She was self-sufficient and head of the household, making sound decisions that benefited those she cared for most.

However, also typically Carrie, she disagreed with a man about the manner in which she taught reading and, as a result, lost her job. Again, she turned to the Bible for direction and felt it was God's will that she marry David Nation, a local minister and widower with a four-year-old daughter.

That marriage took the little family, which still included Mother Gloyd, to Texas, where, because of David's limited abilities to generate an income, Carrie became financially independent by operating a hotel/boardinghouse/dining room. The nonstop work of feeding and cleaning for guests in the thirty-eight rooms took every ounce of energy she had. Yet Carrie began weekly visits to neighboring businesses to collect food and clothing for the less fortunate. Anyone who came to the hotel in need of a meal received one regardless of whether he or she could afford to pay. Many a tired soul spent the night in a warm and comfortable bed at no charge.

However, life in Texas in the 1880s was still a pretty rough place. Like elsewhere in the South, race issues created deep and violent divisions between otherwise compatible neighbors. Those who were most unhappy with the outcome of the Civil War were known as the Jaybirds, but those who were comfortable with and promoted equality between the races were known as Peckerwoods.

Both David and Carrie believed very much in the equality of all people regardless of race or gender. Unfortunately, those beliefs put them in growing danger. After a gang of Jaybirds severely beat David, the Nations decided it was time to leave Texas. The free soil of Kansas was calling. Carrie saw it more as God calling. Kansas was the first state in the Union to have a constitutional amendment outlawing the manufacture and sale of alcohol.

Medicine Lodge and the Christian church where David was to become pastor was their home beginning in 1889. For the first time in her married life, Carrie could be a homemaker and serve in the role of pastor's wife. Her abundant energy and generosity to others flourished in this role. She started sewing circles to make clothing for needy children. She collected food and other items for families who had nothing. She made sure that children who otherwise would have received nothing found an appropriate gift waiting for them on Christmas morning. She taught Sunday school and ministered to those in jail.

"To be womanly," Carrie wrote, "means strength of character, virtue and power for good."

From each of these ministerial outlets, she heard stories of desperation and unhappiness that resulted from alcohol abuse. She prayed diligently in private and voiced her concerns at church and to community leaders, elected officials, and anyone who would listen. Very few did listen, however, either because of their laissez-faire attitude about alcohol use in a state where it was outlawed or because of Carrie's incessant badgering approach to the issue.

Throughout this time, Carrie's faith and religious fervor grew significantly. In Texas she believed she had received a vision from God. She spent endless hours on her knees at home, chanting and praising the Lord. Her greeting to anyone she met on the street became "Do you love God?" At church she became more vocal, openly criticizing anyone she believed drank or who was not pious in dress. Young people received lectures on the immorality of buggy riding, and children in her Sunday school classes received a trip to the cemetery for lessons on hell's fire.

David soon lost his job and they moved again, ever so briefly, to Holton, Kansas, where Carrie became even more outspoken. She often took the pulpit from her husband when dissatisfied with his sermons. She criticized the choir for robes that were too colorful and admonished women who wore hats that Carrie considered extravagant. Within a few months, this church, too, decided it was time for a new pastor. The Nations returned to Medicine Lodge and David began to practice law.

She helped organize a chapter of the Women's Christian Temperance Union in Medicine Lodge, and although not its president, Carrie certainly became its most vocal and active member. This was about the time she started spelling her name "Carry" instead of Carrie. She believed that Carry A. Nation would indeed "carry a nation" away from the immorality of alcohol.

At first she and other ladies began praying peacefully although vocally outside the saloons of Medicine Lodge. There were seven in town and the WCTU's goal was to close each and every one. A bar owned by Henry Durst was first on their list. Twice a day, Carry led prayer vigils outside.

Carry soon became bolder by actually entering the saloons. She began by greeting those inside with the words "Good morning, destroyer of men's souls." Then, standing in the middle of the saloon, Carry would sing hymns at the top of her lungs or fall to her knees calling for God to vanquish the world of alcohol and its evils. Outside, her colleagues would beat drums and sing along.

At any restaurant, pharmacy, or general store where she suspected alcohol was in the back rooms, Carry made her presence known, pushing past male employees into private rooms where, indeed, she often found alcohol. Carry's first "smashing" occurred on December 11, 1894, when the ten-gallon barrel of whiskey she discovered was rolled out into the street. As a crowd gathered and the local sheriff tried to calm the situation, Carry grabbed the sledgehammer offered by a temperance colleague. In one swoop, the barrel splintered and the women set fire to its contents, singing and praising God for the incident that was later dubbed the "Petticoat Riot."

"Whiskey," she would say, "is a cruel tyrant." Despite her radical methods, a large number of men were touched by Carry's convictions and her sincere efforts to improve their lives. Many indeed gave up drinking and lived productive lives, providing for their families and contributing to the community.

Within a few weeks of the Petticoat Riot, all seven saloons were gone from Medicine Lodge. As a result, the illegal alcohol businesses in nearby Kiowa flourished. It's rumored that even David Nation made a few visits to Kiowa.

Throughout all of this, the relationship between Carry and David, which had never been strong, began to suffer. They moved for a short period to a homestead on the Cherokee Strip in Oklahoma, where things went as badly as before, and soon they were back in Medicine Lodge. From the earliest days in their marriage, Carry had doubts about David's religious convictions. Even then, their only arguments were about matters of faith and interpretation of scripture.

In June 1900, as word of Kiowa's flourishing alcohol economy spread, Carry quietly decided to take her saloon closures to the next level. Over a period of a few days, she loaded her buggy with stones and bricks, each individually wrapped in newspaper. On the pretense of visiting friends near Kiowa, off she went, singing praises as her buggy passed through the peaceful Kansas Flint Hills.

Shortly after eight thirty the next morning, the melee began. Upon entering the first saloon and with the force of any major league pitcher, Carry lobbed armloads of rocks at bottles of alcohol, mirrors, and windows. When the rocks were gone, she grabbed billiard balls and sticks, continuing her destructive attack on tables, chairs, and other furnishings.

Carry was on her third saloon before law enforcement physically intervened. Although she certainly could have been arrested for destruction of property, the town leaders didn't quite know what to do. By arresting her, they would be openly recognizing that numerous businesses were illegally selling alcohol. But even worse, by arresting her, they feared an invasion of Christian women who supported Carry's cause.

Fear of the WCTU was the deciding factor. Carry was let go with a warning and told never to return to Kiowa. Later, as her destruction continued, law enforcement would not be so lenient. Before she died, Carry Nation was arrested forty-one times and stood trial four times. In each trial, claims were made that Carry was insane, that no sound-minded individual would behave in such an irrational manner.

That Carry's mother, Mary, had since been placed and died in an asylum near Nevada, Missouri, did not help her case. Carry compared herself to Moses, who destroyed the tablet containing the Ten Commandments, so enraged was he by idolatry. Like the abolitionist John Brown, whom Carry considered a joyful influence on her work, she declared she was entirely sane. The courts agreed.

Throughout Kansas, and certainly other communities around the United States, frustration about the illegal sale of alcohol was growing. Saloon smashing similar to Carry's single-handed attack on Kiowa occurred from coast to coast, even in places where alcohol was legal. Carry and the women of Kansas were not alone in their efforts. Nor was Carry the first to grab a hatchet to improve her destructive capabilities.

David Nation spent the Christmas holidays of 1900 with his brother in Neosho County, Kansas, allowing Carry time to pray and prepare for her next big adventure, the one that would throw her into the national spotlight.

Arriving alone in Wichita on the evening of December 27, Carry visited a number of saloons and decided that the one housed inside the Carey Hotel, easily the most elaborate in the city, was where she would begin her attack.

Back in her room, she prayed much of the night, but also took a few moments to reinforce her cane by tying an iron rod to it. She had learned in Kiowa that rocks smash only once, so something sturdier that she could keep in her hand at all times would be more effective.

Again, she began early in the morning when the bar had the fewest customers. Was her timing based on a desire to do the most damage before being physically stopped? Or did she choose the early hours to minimize the potential for hurting others? Many believed it was her concern for fellow human beings that caused her to choose the morning hours. Maybe she was just an early riser.

Within minutes, the Carey Hotel was in shambles with glass shards everywhere, liquor flowing from broken bottles and barrels, furniture destroyed, and holes in the plastered walls. This time, however, law enforcement didn't take her actions so light-heartedly. Carry was arrested and spent nearly three weeks in jail.

But the conditions of her imprisonment were a greater violation than any destruction she had caused so far. Besides the overall filthy environment that included bedbugs and lice in the mattress and no blankets or pillows in December, Carry was denied access to supporters and even her husband, who came to her rescue. A fellow inmate, they were told, had smallpox and the entire jail was quarantined.

Of course, that was not the case and finally on January 12, 1901, under orders from the Kansas Supreme Court, Carry was released from jail. Nine days later, she was back at it, and for the first time, Carry Nation's arsenal included a hatchet.

The hatchet was used liberally in another raid in Wichita, in Topeka, and in just about every community of any size over the next sixteen months. Quickly bar owners began to defend their property. Carry was the target of much of the brutality, even when accompanied by supporters and members of the WCTU. She was punched in the face, was horsewhipped, had a chair broken over her head, was pelted with rotten eggs, and more. A Wichita bar owner held a gun to her head until she left the premises.

Soon the comparisons began between Carry Nation and John Brown, the Kansas abolitionist who was executed for his efforts, somewhat violent at times, to end slavery. Her vigilante approach to solving the problem began only when acceptable forms of protest and communication failed to produce results. And like John Brown, Carry was fully prepared to die for her cause.

It's quite possible that plans to murder Carry were behind the telegram she received about the deplorable conditions in Hope, a small community about twenty miles south of Abilene. Because her work would soon take her to Abilene, Carry telegraphed back that she would indeed stop in Hope on the way.

Finding no one to greet her at the train station, Carry checked into the only hotel, with plans for a good night's sleep. Late in the night, she received a knock at her door. A gruff male voice announced that she had visitors downstairs. Because of the stench of cigarette smoke outside her door—a warning from God, Carry claimed—she refused to open her door. The individual continued to cajole her into coming downstairs until Carry, now armed with her hatchet, began to raise her voice and threaten to scream.

A few minutes later, looking out her window, Carry saw two unidentifiable men emerge from the hotel and disappear into the shadows.

That didn't deter Carry. Her "hatchetation" campaign assaulted towns around Kansas and throughout the Midwest. During a particular nasty three-week attack on Topeka, including the Senate saloon in the state capitol building, she engaged in shouting matches with nearly every elected official, including the governor in his own office. Reporters witnessing the exchange commented on Carry's excellent command of logic and the English language. On more than one occasion, she shouted, "You wouldn't give me the vote, so I had to use a rock."

Through it all, David Nation had attempted to be at her side, bailing her out of jail, defending her in court, and even handling some of her correspondence. However, in 1901, David filed for divorce, citing desertion and humiliation among the many charges. The divorce papers also stated that Carry was gone so often that she left "her true responsibilities of womanhood unfulfilled." Two years later, David died at age seventy-three. He is buried in the Medicine Lodge Highland Cemetery.

Although she continued her campaign against alcohol with all of her vocal and physical might until her death on June 2, 1911, Carry's entire hatcheting career only lasted about sixteen months. Her most logical reasoning, according to those around her and those who have studied her work, is that the use of a hatchet had generated enough national attention that the wheels were put in motion that eventually ended in Prohibition.

Although she was threatened, jailed, and beaten during her eleven-year crusade, she was also welcomed as a hero, a "defender of the home," and a true gift from God. So is that who Carry Nation really was, a woman whose heart had been broken by alcohol? Or was she just an overbearing female who found temperance as her pathway to history?

CHAPTER 10

John Brown

Was this legendary abolitionist really a mad-dog killer inflamed by much of the violence in pre–Civil War Kansas? Or was he simply a spirited leader who believed in the equality of all human beings?

John Brown was fifty-five years old when he came to Kansas and stayed for just about ten months. However, in that short time, he did more to galvanize the free-state cause in Kansas and accelerate the national movement to end slavery via the Civil War than anyone of his time.

Many believed him to be insane. Certainly his behavior throughout much of his life was not in step with the mainstream by any means. His leadership in the brutal and unorthodox slaying of five proslavery men in Kansas really pushed that envelope. Although shocking to the sensibilities of Northerner and Southerner alike, the attack in Kansas elevated the name John Brown to the national stage.

John Brown

Northerners began to listen more closely to his "Do unto others" message with regard to slavery and the treatment of all ethnic minorities.

Southerners were infuriated by the man, his family, and his overt slap-in-the-face to their entire culture. It was heresy, treason, and simply ungentlemanly conduct.

Indeed the unconscionable and ghastly events carried out in the moonless hours of May 24–25, 1856, were attention-getters, driving some who participated in the activities that night to the true brink of insanity. But had the events not happened, would Kansas have entered the Union as a free state? Would the inevitable Civil War over states' rights and slavery have been postponed?

And of lesser consequence, why was John Brown never prosecuted for the lives he took on that spring night? Did he, or did he not, lift the sword that dismembered five men on the banks of Pottawatomie Creek?

As early as 1817, when he was just seventeen years old, John Brown was already taking an active role in protecting and liberating slaves. He was born into a family of Calvinistic Puritans who might have had relatives on the *Mayflower,* and his earliest memories included his father's close friendship with a black farmer who lived near their Connecticut home.

When John was just five, the family moved to Hudson, Ohio. The new location allowed the Browns to interact with American Indians on a daily basis, and unlike most whites moving west of the Alleghenies at this time, the Browns did not feel threatened by their presence. The Brown family practice of the Golden Rule, which transcends all religions in teaching that we treat others as we would like to be treated, included American Indians as well as slaves.

John Brown lost his mother when he was just eight years old, and with five siblings, he often had to stay out of school and help at home or in his father's tannery. His father's work in the cattle business required that John, as young as twelve years old, herd cattle several hundred miles for delivery to customers. It was then, when out in the world alone, that he first witnessed physical and verbal abuses of slaves.

By the time he was seventeen, John had already considered, then dropped his plan to enter the ministry. Instead, he and a brother began their own tannery a few miles from their father's. One day the brothers were approached by a runaway slave who needed food and shelter while escaping those searching for him. They gladly obliged.

Situated between Cleveland and Akron, Hudson was an active stop on the Underground Railroad, or as John Brown called it, the "Subterranean Pass Way." It's estimated that as many as two thousand slaves a year followed the Underground Railroad through Ohio prior to the Civil War. Whether the Brown family knew that as they chose Hudson when moving West remains unknown.

John built a hiding place for slaves in the hay barn and was often out in the middle of the night transporting these Southern fugitives from one safe house to the next. It was not uncommon for five or six slaves a night to receive a meal and safe lodging in the Brown barn.

Such activities violated both federal and state laws, representing the first time John Brown knowingly broke the law by participating in criminal acts. However, Hudson was just the first place across the growing United States where John Brown would help slaves find their way to freedom. And it was not the last place he would knowingly commit a crime.

For such a remarkable and legendary conclusion to John Brown's life, much of it was really very ordinary. In June 1820, he married Dianthe Lusk and together they had seven children, two of whom died at an early age. Dianthe died in childbirth in August 1832, and by June 1833, John Brown had remarried a woman named Mary Day. Between the two marriages, John fathered twenty children.

Although he might have been successful at leading slaves to freedom, deterring proslavery forces in Kansas, and contributing to the start of the Civil War, John Brown was a lousy businessman and provider for his large family of children. His family was among society's poorest of poor everywhere they lived, often surviving on corn mush, potatoes, and little else. Although disease and death were much more common among children of the nineteenth century, their poor diet and living conditions surely contributed to illnesses that eventually took nine of the twenty children John fathered. In one week in September 1843, John and Mary lost four children. Three more would later die in an effort to end slavery.

Those who knew and worked with John Brown throughout the 1830s and '40s regarded him as exceedingly honest and trustworthy. Yet, John Brown was equally stubborn. In any business he attempted, from operating his tannery to exporting wool to farming, he might have been more successful had he been more flexible on his pricing or his expectations of others. When he was forty-nine years old, he filed for bankruptcy.

Through it all, John Brown's abolitionist beliefs only grew stronger. When not directly assisting runaway slaves in his home, he would send what little money he had to organizations that provided assistance. He read newspaper articles, attended lectures, and wrote letters to political and business leaders expressing in no uncertain terms his opinion on the matter of slavery.

And he began to form a plan.

In November 1847, John Brown's path crossed that of Frederick Douglass, the escaped slave-turned-abolitionist leader in New York. Douglass later wrote of this meeting in his newspaper, the *North Star:* "Though a white gentleman, (Brown) is in sympathy a black man, and as deeply interested in our cause, as though his own soul had been pierced with the iron of slavery."

Yet John Brown was not your typical abolitionist. Although most abolitionists believed slavery was wrong, they still believed that blacks were inferior and, as such, didn't want to interact with them. Many abolitionists supported the idea that slaves should be returned to Africa or at least deported from the United States.

Brown believed that all races were equal and that when freed, blacks should be integrated into American society and contribute to the nation's growth and discourse. He had hopes of founding a black school and went so far as to help build an all-black community in upstate New York near Lake Placid called North Elba. Here the Brown family, which now included many adult children and their spouses and children, lived proudly with free blacks and escaped slaves.

Brown was different from abolitionists in another, more significant manner. Most abolitionists were nonviolent people. Although he had not yet become violent, John admired slave rebels like Nat Turner, who in 1831 led six other slaves on a nighttime killing spree through Southampton County, Virginia. With swords and axes, they killed fifty-five white people—men, women, and children—before they disappeared into the nearby hills and were eventually caught and hanged.

This is the John Brown who was coming into being in May 1854, when Congress approved the Kansas-Nebraska Act. Basically the act repealed the Missouri Compromise of 1820, which restricted the expansion of slavery north of the thirty-sixth parallel. At the same time, the Kansas-Nebraska Act allowed for "popular sovereignty," which meant that anyone living in the territory at the time of the vote could determine whether to allow slavery in the state.

The Browns hated the Kansas-Nebraska Act. "Hate" is perhaps too mild of a word. John became outraged, livid, and consumed with the very distinct possibility that slavery could spread not only to Kansas and Nebraska, but to any state in the Union.

By October 1854, three of John Brown's grown sons—Owen, Frederick, and Salmon—left North Elba for Kansas, arriving in April 1855. They settled eight miles west of Osawatomie, a small community about sixty miles south of Kansas City. Within a few months, two more Brown children—Jason and John Jr.—joined their brothers with their families.

John Brown himself couldn't decide whether to go to Kansas. He could make considerable contributions to the cause by staying in the East, working with the Underground Railroad, and certainly attempting to earn an income to support Mary and the younger children who remained at home.

Finally John Brown asked that his black neighbors in North Elba make the decision. They voted overwhelmingly for him to go and sent money and weapons along with him. Making stops in Cleveland, Akron, Chicago, and other communities along the way, John received additional financial support, with which he bought swords, guns, ammunition, a horse and wagon, and other supplies. On October 7 John, along with his sixteen-year-old son, Oliver, and son-in-law Henry Thompson, arrived at the little settlement they called Brown's Station.

Nothing about what was happening in Kansas at this time is something to be proud of, in a local, national, or historical setting. It was simply violent, greedy, self-serving, and incorrigibly destructive.

The opening of the territory for settlement certainly attracted a fair number of families and individuals simply looking for adventure or a fresh start in uncharted land. Buffalo Bill Cody's family was among those who had no political agenda. They simply wanted to leave Iowa and memories of the tragic death of a child there.

However, a large majority who rushed to Kansas were motivated by this one dominant political issue that threatened to tear a nation in two. Several historical studies place the number of unregistered, out-of-state voters in the first territorial election at 80 percent.

Of course, it would be too simple and naive to categorize those people as either proslavery or free-staters, although many at the time tried to do so. It was much more complicated than that.

For example, John Brown wanted to abolish slavery everywhere and believed that blacks and whites could and should live together harmoniously. He was certainly a free-stater. Others who voted for a free Kansas wanted a Kansas free of anyone other than whites. They didn't want an American Indian, a slave, or anyone who was not white and Christian to live in Kansas.

On the proslavery side, there were people like David Rice Atchison, a Missouri slave owner and state senator who fully embraced the concept of slavery in both moral and economic terms. He and others like him believed themselves superior to blacks and hoped to benefit financially from their labor as the railroads moved west.

Also on the proslavery side were low-income, poorly educated Southern whites who were paid by wealthy plantation owners to move to Kansas to influence the vote. These individuals probably believed themselves superior to blacks but really didn't care one way or the other about what happened in Kansas.

Therefore, most of those who came to Kansas were already emotionally charged, some radically so, but all very passionate. Mix it up with free-flowing alcohol, easily accessible firearms, and political rhetoric that encouraged voting with a knife and revolver, and it's remarkable that even more lives were not lost.

A day free of death and violence as a direct result of the pending vote on slavery was a rare occurrence in the border area of Kansas from 1854 to the end of the Civil War. Homes and crops were burned, businesses looted and destroyed, churches and schools desecrated. Newspaper owners and journalists were common targets, as were ministers and politicians. Tarring and feathering became a regular occurrence.

Record keeping from the time period was spotty at best, but scholarly studies agree that the majority of violence was instigated by proslavery forces and that free-staters were the target. Southerners considered the abolitionists cowards. With the rare exception, abolitionists simply did not engage in violence.

It was equally rare that anyone was ever arrested or prosecuted for these crimes.

Of course, the Browns were right in the middle of it all. John was appointed a captain in the First Brigade of Kansas Volunteers. He and John Jr. were leaders of the Liberty Guards, who defended Lawrence during the skirmishes of November and December 1855, called the Wakarusa War.

The Browns liberated two slaves who had been brought to the Lawrence area. They organized meetings, gave lectures, and attended any number of events that bolstered the concept of equality and the abolitionist viewpoint.

The highly visible and vocal manner in which the Browns held their position undoubtedly infuriated the area's proslavery leaders. Although they had not yet broken any laws, one proslavery judge named Sterling Cato issued a warrant in April 1856 for the arrest of John Brown and his sons.

This, and the beating of an elected free-state official, was the final straw that sent John Brown over the edge. He had come to Kansas looking for a fight and believed for months that he was fully engaged in war. Now the battle had become personal.

The selection of his victims, encouraged by son Jason, was based on those present in "court" the day Sterling Cato issued his warrants and other proslavery thugs who had personally challenged the Browns.

There were eight who set out together on the afternoon of May 23, 1856. The group included John Brown and his sons,

Frederick, Salmon, Oliver, and Owen, his son-in-law Henry Thompson, and two allies, Theodore Weiner and James Townsley. Oliver, just sixteen, and his brother Frederick were not enthusiastic about this plan and participated only at the direct command of their father.

On Saturday night, about ten o'clock, the group approached the cabin of James Doyle, killing two barking dogs. Under the pretense of asking directions, they convinced Doyle to open the door. They stormed in, taking Doyle and his two oldest sons prisoners. The three were led into the nearby woods, where Owen and Salmon Brown attacked them with swords. John fired one shot into the skull of James Doyle.

A few hundred yards away, Allen Wilkinson and his wife were soundly sleeping when, just before midnight, they were awakened by a knock at the door from someone asking directions. Not only did the marauders take his life in a most violent manner, but they also took horses and saddles.

By this time it was after midnight. It was Sunday, the Sabbath, a day of worship and praise, or at least it always had been in the Brown household.

Instead, John Brown, who had once aspired to the ministry, led the group to the home of James Harris in search of one of their primary antagonists, Henry Sherman. Sherman was not to be found, but instead, the Brown party was satisfied with his brother William, who had also verbally thrashed the Browns for the family's political and moral beliefs on slavery.

The next morning William Sherman's body was found mutilated and partially submerged in the Pottawatomie Creek.

Within hours, the Brown cabins were all burned to the ground by proslavery guerrillas, and the Brown women fled to safety at the home of John Brown's half-sister in Osawatomie. For the next three months, the men hid out on the prairie and in nearby woods, occasionally visiting their loved ones in Osawatomie under the cover of darkness.

They participated in numerous little skirmishes and guerrilla warfare on their enemies. Osawatomie was attacked and burned by proslavery forces on August 30, but only after the men under John Brown's command made a commendable effort at defending the community. Just prior to the battle, twenty-five-year-old Frederick Brown was killed by a proslavery volunteer.

For the first time, the proslavery forces met resistance and were not only shocked, but also occasionally surrendered. At the same time, the unprecedented boldness and overt defiance by John Brown's men, a group that at times reached thirty or more, infuriated Southerners that summer of 1856.

The rhetoric and violence in Kansas escalated further, but it would have to do so without John Brown. Although his sons stayed to fight the good fight, John Brown decided to return east to his wife and younger children and continue his abolitionist efforts on a different plane.

In all of the violence of Bleeding Kansas, only eight proslavery people were murdered. John Brown was responsible for five of those. Although he did not participate in the May 1856 murders, John Brown Jr. broke under the stress and violence of it all. He was imprisoned and later freed but was never considered "right" again. Oliver and Watson Brown died excruciating deaths at Harpers Ferry.

And yet John Brown's mark was made, not only in Kansas, but on the national agenda. The basis of his plan, inspired by Nat Turner's slave rebellion of 1831 and revealed to Frederick Douglass in November 1847, had been only partially implemented on that May night on the Kansas prairie.

It would come to full fruition at a place called Harpers Ferry, in what is now West Virginia, on October 16, 1859. Although the raid on the federal arsenal with plans to free and arm slaves failed, and John Brown was hanged on December 2, 1859, the freedom ball was already rolling. Two years later, shots were fired at Fort Sumter and the Civil War was under way.

CHAPTER 11

Amelia Earhart's Return to Atchison, Kansas

D id the pioneer aviator plan her own disappearance and live out a natural life under a new identity?

Few women in the world, certainly in North America, have generated as much intrigue, spirited debate, and all-around argument over the circumstances surrounding their life and death as Amelia Earhart, the famous pilot who was attempting to fly around the world when, in 1937, she mysteriously disappeared somewhere in the South Pacific.

Dozens of theories have been debated over the years and hundreds of factors that might have contributed to the plane's disappearance have surfaced. Researchers of all calibers have combed the remote islands of the South Pacific, sifted through countless government files and records, and documented conversations with nearly everyone who ever knew or worked with Amelia Earhart and her navigator, Fred Noonan, in an attempt to piece together an acceptable account of the flight that ended not in setting a world record, but in creating a mystery that may never be answered.

However, in Amelia's hometown of Atchison, Kansas, the decades of speculation have simply increased the community's dedication to protecting her reputation and integrity while helping the curious understand how her childhood years here contributed to the accomplishments and inspiration she gave to the world.

Amelia Mary Earhart was born July 24, 1897, at the home of her maternal grandparents, Alfred and Amelia Otis, at 223 North Terrace Street in Atchison. The house sits on a bluff facing east over the Missouri River and the expansive plains of northern Missouri beyond. Even today it is an inspirational view, one that surely contributed to the wanderlust and sense of adventure in this naturally curious child.

Two and half years later, Amelia's sister, Muriel, was born, and the girls were constant companions and confidants. Muriel and Amelia, nicknamed Pidge and Meelie, experienced a childhood quite different from that of most young women of the time. Both their mother and father were progressive for the time and very committed to the girls' education. The girls were encouraged to learn from hands-on experiences and were allowed a good deal of freedom in their play. Amelia rode her bicycle with the boys and played football. She is said to have belly flopped on her sled, shot a rifle, and ridden horses straddle.

Their grandmother, however, did not share such a liberal perspective of proper young ladies' behavior. Amelia in particular

A number of people in Atchison, Kansas, believe that Amelia Earhart returned to her family home here long after she disappeared in the South Pacific.

was frequently chastised by her grandmother, to which the girl often responded with one of her more famous and revealing quotes: "Oh no, Grandmother. Little girls should be allowed to do anything little boys can do."

Amelia and Muriel's mother, also named Amelia, was a record setter herself, having been the first woman to ride horseback to the top of Pike's Peak. Their father, Edward Earhart, was a claims attorney for the Rock Island Railroad. Accounts from numerous sources indicate that he was not particularly successful at this job and may have even had an alcohol problem, all of which surely contributed to Amelia and Edward's divorce when the girls were in their teens.

Although the family moved from Kansas City, Kansas, to Des Moines, Iowa, and back and places in between, the girls often stayed for long periods with their grandparents in Atchison. Alfred Otis was a successful attorney specializing in issues of the railroad and was, therefore, a respected and affluent member of the community. As a result, the girls had unfettered access to books, resources, travel, and stimulating conversation.

The property the Otis family owned was several acres adjacent to a city park and included outbuildings, trees, and a huge garden. The girls explored every nook and cranny, and were as captivated by the bugs and earthworms in the garden as they were the badgers, foxes, squirrels, and rodents in the barns and fields.

At one point, after having seen a roller coaster at the 1904 World's Fair in St. Louis, the girls took it upon themselves to build their own roller coaster–like device. Amelia took the first run and immediately lost control on the first curve, flying off into the yard and crashing a few feet away. In picking herself up off the ground, she is said to have shouted to her sister, "Oh, Pidge, it's just like flying!"

Although a reconstruction of this contraption is a part of the Amelia Earhart Birthplace Museum in Atchison, there is some thought that the roller coaster might actually have been built in the backyard of their home in Kansas City.

All of this supports the concept that the roughly twelve years that Amelia spent in Atchison not only were her formative years as a child, but also contributed significantly to the innate strength, intelligence, and fearlessness that led her along paths that so few had traveled before.

However, it was while living in Des Moines that the Earhart family attended the 1907 Iowa State Fair and Amelia saw her first airplane. She later recounted in numerous articles "It was a thing of rusty wire and wood and not at all interesting. . . ."

But this was just four years after the Wright brothers' first flight at Kitty Hawk, an important fact to remember about the infant stages of aircraft design when criticism arises of Amelia's earliest and less fortunate attempts in aviation.

It was thirteen years later, in December 1920, while Amelia was living in California with her parents, that she accompanied her father to an air show at Daugherty Field in Long Beach. A pilot by the name of Frank Hawks took her up for a ten-minute ride in an open-cockpit biplane. Later she recalled, "By the time I had got two or three hundred feet off the ground, I knew I had to fly."

Less than a week later, Amelia took her first flying lesson and within a very few years, the name Amelia Earhart would forever be linked to aviation history.

Amelia's grandparents, Alfred and Amelia Otis, died when the family was living in Chicago, and it's quite possible that the girls returned to Atchison on occasion visiting other family and friends in the area. However, in June 1935 Amelia returned to Kansas to speak at the Kansas State Editorial Association Convention in Atchison.

By this time, she had already become the first woman to cross the Atlantic in an airplane and later the first woman to fly solo across the Atlantic; to fly from Honolulu to the US mainland; to set numerous altitude records; and so much more. She was an author, writing aviation columns for several publications, and a regular guest at the White House. She designed clothing and luggage and was a widely sought-after public figure. Her name and face were recognized around the world.

That June the people of Atchison welcomed her back with a parade and other events in her honor. She stayed with her cousins, the Challises, just two houses south of the home where she had lived with her grandparents.

This was the last documented time Amelia Earhart visited Atchison, although some in this community strongly believe she returned to her grandparents' home, the museum that now bears her name at 223 North Terrace Street, as late as the early 1990s.

On June 1, 1937, Amelia Earhart departed Miami on her most ambitious goal, one sought by most of the great aviators of the time. She, along with navigator Fred Noonan, was hoping to fly around the world, approximately twenty-nine thousand miles, a feat that had been talked about but never attempted.

Despite a few problems with inaccurate maps and a few weather delays, the flight went along fairly well. On July 1 from Lae, New Guinea, the two prepared for the most difficult leg of the trip—a 2,556-mile, eighteen-hour flight to Howland Island in the middle of the Pacific Ocean. The US Coast Guard cutter *Itasca* was stationed near Howland Island to receive radio transmissions. Two other US ships were stationed along the flight path, all lights on, as beacons for Amelia and her navigator.

The twin-engine Lockheed Electra, stripped of all unnecessary weight to carry extra fuel, took off at ten a.m. local time. They soon encountered bad weather, which made navigation by the stars nearly impossible. Near dawn, the crew on the *Itasca* began picking up transmissions from the Electra, but apparently Amelia could not hear the return transmissions.

At 7:42 a.m., the *Itasca* recorded the message, "We must be on you, but we cannot see you. Fuel is running low. Been unable to reach you by radio. We are flying at 1,000 feet." The crew replied, but there was no response. About an hour later, the crew heard Amelia's voice for the last time: "We are running north and south," she said, and nothing further was heard.

The ensuing search and rescue effort involving the US Coast Guard, Navy, and Air Force continued until July 19 and covered more than 250,000 square miles of ocean. No sign of Amelia, her navigator, or the Lockheed Electra was found.

In a letter left to her husband, George Putnam, and later published in his book *Soaring Wings,* as well as other sources, she had written, "Please know I am quite aware of the hazards. I want to do it because I want to do it. Women must try to do things as men have tried. When they fail, their failure must be but a challenge to others."

The numerous theories regarding the disappearance of the Lockheed Electra and its two famous passengers have ranged from the simplistic to the absurd. The most simple and obvious, of course, is that the overcast skies created impossible navigation conditions, the plane was seriously off course, it crashed in the ocean, and its passengers did not survive. That is also the most widely accepted theory.

In that same vein is that the plane and its passengers made it safely to some remote island far off course and the passengers perished while waiting to be rescued.

Others believe that Amelia was secretly participating in espionage of Japanese installations in the region at the behest of President Franklin Roosevelt. It was well known that Roosevelt engaged civilians in such activities prior to the advent of World

War II. Perhaps the Japanese forced the plane to land and took the passengers prisoner, where they died in captivity. Accounts from prisoner of war camps on Saipan during WWII report two, possibly as many as three, Caucasian women being held on the island.

But a third theory is the one filled with the most intrigue and potential for conspiracy, one that many of the people who knew Amelia best believe was possible for this woman who had never followed convention or others' expectations.

Is it possible that Amelia Earhart, tired of the public spectacle that her lifetime of achievements had brought upon her and her family, planned her disappearance and, working with the federal government, created a new identity where she could live the remainder of her life out of the public eye?

"Some people come here and say 'Oh, Amelia would never do that,' and I say 'Oh, yes she would,'" says Louise Foudray, caretaker of the Amelia Earhart Birthplace Museum. "Amelia Earhart definitely had a mind of her own and exercised it when she lived here."

According to Louise, just before she departed on the world flight, Amelia told her friend and personal photographer, Albert Bresnik, "When I come back, I'm going to live a life away from the public eye."

Of course, the only way an individual of her international fame and accomplishments could have done that would be to take on a new identity. And from what Louise has learned over the years, "that sounds like Amelia."

Louise Foudray has lived in Atchison since the 1960s and, like most residents of the community, simply believed that Amelia Earhart and Fred Noonan crashed in the ocean in 1937. But that, she said, is the easy answer, and nothing about Amelia Earhart would have been that easy.

"But we believed that if she was still living, she would probably come back to Atchison for a visit, so everyone was always on the lookout for someone who might be suspicious," says Louise.

One woman who was a frequent volunteer at the county museum in the 1960s often told the story of a mysterious woman who came in on occasion and made broad, sweeping statements that Amelia was still alive and living in New Jersey.

"There was certainly no proof of it, but for some people, there was that sentiment that Amelia was still living and it was supposed to be a secret, although not that much of a secret to some people," says Louise.

Another oft-repeated story comes from one of several visits Amelia's sister, Muriel, made to Atchison over the years. A local acquaintance approached Muriel with questions about the disappearance and Muriel's answer was, "Why don't they leave my sister alone?"

Was Muriel speaking in the present tense or the past tense when she made this response?

In 1984 the house in which Amelia was born was purchased by the Ninety-Nines, an international organization of licensed women pilots. Amelia was a founding member in 1929 and was the organization's first president.

The organization began efforts to restore the home to the time when Amelia and Muriel lived there and in 1987 hired Louise Foudray as the home's full-time caretaker. Louise does not consider herself a researcher, but in more than twenty years of living in and operating the home where Amelia's personality came into being, and talking with thousands of visitors with various theories, she can certainly be considered an expert on the life of this famous, yet in the end, very mysterious woman.

"In the beginning Amelia was not the best pilot, but in the early years of aviation, everyone was learning. She did make some mistakes. I have talked with mechanics and others who worked with her. They said Amelia was very intelligent and planned everything down to the last detail, that she would not leave on a flight until she planned alternate landing places, she always had several backup plans," says Louise.

Unlike the image portrayed in the 1994 TV movie *Amelia Earhart: The Final Flight,* starring Diane Keaton, the people who worked with Amelia told Louise that Amelia was always very eager to ask questions and learn every detail of the airplane. The image created in that movie suggests that Amelia was argumentative and hard to work with, "and I don't believe that was the case," says Louise.

Over the years, several members of the Amelia Earhart Research Society have visited the home in Atchison and have made presentations at the birthday events each July. Louise has traveled to their conferences in Colorado and California and at Purdue University, as well as one research trip to the Marshall Islands.

From these experiences, Lou has developed a greater respect for Amelia's intelligence and fearlessness.

"She was a strong scientist and mathematician. The lack of fear came from planning and from being careful," Lou says. "I agree with what many people have told me about her, that in the beginning she may not have been a very good pilot, but by 1937, she was probably the best pilot in the world."

The Ninety-Nines explicitly do not endorse any theory about the disappearance, yet simply encourage reasonable discourse and an appreciation of what Amelia accomplished for women and for aviation science around the world.

Louise Foudray supports that position as well; however, when she began working at the museum, she pledged to herself to keep an eye out for anyone who might be suspicious—just in case.

"I've had some visitors here with whom I wish I would have been a little more bold and intrusive in asking questions of them," Louise says. "There was one lady who came who was very familiar with the house and asked a lot of questions. A few days later, she called back with more questions and then she told me she was Amelia Earhart's daughter."

Amelia did not have any children of her own at the time of her disappearance, so the only scenario that would have given Amelia children was if she had indeed lived past July 1937.

However, more suspect than the woman claiming to be Amelia's daughter was a visitor Louise recalls from the early 1990s. This woman was quite elderly and stooped from age. She was dressed well and accompanied by two young men wearing suits.

"As I was leading a group on the tour, this woman and her companions broke off from the tour and she was looking around, looking for something," says Louise. "I heard her say, 'I know it's here; I just can't remember where.'"

At the time, the floors in the home were being repaired and the hallway was blocked that led to the formal dining room, a distinct oval room with intricate stained-glass windows. It was hidden from view on both the inside and the outside. A room like that would be a vivid memory of anyone who had ever lived in or visited the home.

"I asked the woman and her companions to return to the group and I would answer any questions about the house at the end of the tour, but instead, I heard one of the men say, 'You're too upset. We better leave now.'"

With that, Louise watched as the young men escorted the elderly woman out the door to a waiting black stretch limousine.

CHAPTER 12

A Fortune Buried on the Family Farm

A re cans of money still buried, just waiting to be discovered, on a farm near Independence, Kansas? And who attempted murder to steal what was not rightfully theirs?

Since the beginning of time, tales of buried and lost treasures have spurred people to extraordinary lengths—some brave, some innovative, some downright stupid—as they have searched for their elusive fortunes.

Kansas is not without its unique fables of riches waiting to be uncovered. As far back as the 1540s, Spanish explorer Francisco Vasquez de Coronado searched for those seven cities of gold on the Kansas plains. The city of El Dorado, Kansas, is so named for that inconclusive escapade.

The Santa Fe Trail, as it makes its nine hundred–mile journey from Independence, Missouri, to New Mexico, is fraught with stories of hard choices people made to leave valuables behind along the trail to travel faster and with less physical burden.

Amanda Lambdin Dowthitt's grave site does not reflect the mystery surrounding her death.

Even the Dalton Gang was thought to have buried $20,000 or more near a bridge across Onion Creek the morning before they met their fate in Coffeyville, Kansas, in October 1892.

But we know with certainty that an elderly woman in Montgomery County, Kansas, was indeed hiding money in cans around her farm outside of Independence as recently as the 1950s. Her name was Amanda Lambdin Dowthitt and she was my great-great-aunt.

Every family has its own legendary figures. Not that we're all related to Daniel Boone or Davy Crockett, but there's always someone who helps define a family, and in our case it was Aunt Amanda. Of course, I could share stories about alleged moonshiners in our family tree and the fun we've had with that over the years, but their actions were in another state, so instead we'll focus on the legend of Aunt Amanda.

Lambdins came to the United States from Ireland and Scotland as early as the late 1600s and by the 1880s had moved as far west as southern Indiana. In the fall of 1881, my great-great-grandfather Wilford Lambdin swapped the farm in Indiana—sight unseen—for a farm in Kansas, about five miles southwest of Independence. The small Kansas community had been built by emigrants from Indiana in 1869, so it's quite possible that Wilford swapped his land with an Indiana neighbor who simply wanted to return home. Otherwise, we don't know what possessed Wilf to make such a trade, unless it was for the simple adventure and challenges of the unknown.

Several of the neighbors in the southern Indiana community of Paoli formed a wagon train and accompanied the Lambdin family to Kansas before heading farther west. The Lambdins making that journey included Wilford and his third wife, along with his sons, Ransom, George, and Elwood. Staying behind in Indiana was his daughter Amanda, who would have been about fifteen at the time.

Amanda stayed in Indiana for about two years living with and working for a local family as a housekeeper. She was paid $1 a week, plus room and board. In 1883 she moved on to Kansas to be with her father, brothers, and stepmom. Whether she made the journey alone or in the company of another wagon train headed west is not known.

Times were more difficult in Kansas than expected. The Lambdin family, as well as their neighbors, ate parched corn and the few wild animals they could shoot or trap. The lack of forestation limited the size and scope of wildlife to an occasional deer or antelope. The birds, however, were abundant on the plains, so that would have been a large part of their diet.

The sons worked on the family farm and hired out to local farmers for a few dollars a month. Amanda worked as hard as the men in the family.

After the Homestead Act of 1862 and at the end of the Civil War, Kansas was a hot destination. Free land was there for those with the fortitude to work it and people came from around the globe motivated by this uniquely American dream of owning land. Think of the books by Laura Ingalls Wilder. She and her family lived here in a little house on the prairie from 1869 to 1871, just a few miles south of where the Lambdin family would settle.

Another who came west was Alex B. Jackson of North Carolina. He started a little business in Independence, where he met and married Amanda Lambdin on March 14, 1888. They had not been married five years when one day, as Alex was working to shoe a horse, he was kicked in the head and died of his injuries in November 1892. He was thirty years old when he died and Amanda, at twenty-six years old, was a widow. They had no children.

By this time, Amanda's brothers had moved on to Arkansas and California, and her father, Wilford, died in 1904. She was alone, but not without resources.

Although it was not as common a practice then as it is today, Alex Jackson had purchased life insurance. Amanda was the benefactor of about $3,000, which in today's money is a little over $70,000. Aunt Amanda was single and wealthy.

Coming from a family of farmers, it was not unusual that Amanda chose to invest her good fortune in more land. She bought eighty acres south of Independence and rented out the land to other farmers.

Her choice of acreage was a good one. Railroads were the fastest means of transportation for people and products, and if a railroad came to town in those days, that community was on a fast track for growth and development. The same was true if the railroad decided they needed to lay tracks through your property.

So when in 1898 the Kansas, Oklahoma Central and Southwestern Railway developed a new route out of Independence headed toward El Paso, Texas, the path cut right through property owned by the widow Amanda Jackson. There are no records remaining of the exact transaction, but it's likely the railroad, which later became the Atchison, Topeka and Santa Fe Railway, made annual long-term payments to the landowners. It was a tidy sum, plus Amanda still had income from the farmers who rented the land from her.

And then, lo and behold, the Independence Gas Company and the Penn Drilling Company found oil and natural gas in Montgomery County in about 1902, some of it right there on that farm owned by Amanda Jackson. Not one to live an extravagant lifestyle, Amanda socked every extra penny away in the bank.

And then the stock market crashed in October 1929, ushering in the Great Depression. Like so many others, Amanda lost everything and struggled for survival in tough economic times. It's reasonable that she and many of her generation never trusted banks again.

In the meantime, she met and married Samuel P. Dowthitt on November 25, 1920. There's not a lot known about Sam and Amanda's life together. By the time they married, Amanda was fifty-four years old and they had no children.

Their marriage lasted not quite twenty years. Samuel Dowthitt died on January 7, 1940.

Now in her seventies, Amanda lived a quiet, simple lifestyle. Although not a member, she attended the Presbyterian Church often enough that when she died, the Presbyterian minister, Rev. John Westin, officiated at her service. County records show that she owned some rental homes in town and sold off a couple of acres of her land to adjoining farmers.

She had a small checking account at the Citizens National Bank in Independence, but she had learned a tough lesson during the Great Depression. Even with the implementation of the Federal Deposit Insurance Corporation, Amanda, like many of her generation, had a hard time believing in the security of banks.

She continued to earn money from the oil and natural gas leases on her farm, from her rental properties, from her tenant farmers, and perhaps from a little pension after Samuel Dowthitt's death. But other than a few dollars deposited in the bank to cover her bills, what was Amanda doing with her money?

The question probably never entered into the consciousness of most people who knew the little widow woman living south of town.

But apparently somebody was watching and wondering what Amanda Lambdin Dowthitt was doing with all of her money.

In May 1954, when Amanda was eighty-eight years old, someone broke into her rural home, and robbed and beat her, leaving her for dead. Evidence indicated that this person or persons were in her home for a number of days searching for money and other valuables.

William F. Lessman was in his first of three terms as Montgomery County sheriff in the spring of 1954. When he arrived on the scene, holes had been punched in the walls and floorboards ripped up in several rooms. Couches, chairs, and mattresses had been sliced open. The contents of cabinets, bookshelves, and desks were dumped everywhere.

The outbuildings had not been spared either. From gardening sheds to chicken coops to the big barn, it was evident that someone had been rummaging and digging and disturbing the otherwise orderly, tidy world of this helpless, innocent woman.

Amanda spent several days in the hospital receiving treatment for her injuries before she was transferred permanently to the Viets Nursing Home for long-term care. Court records indicate that on June 22 she was judged incompetent to handle her own affairs.

Amanda's closest blood relatives were the three children of her brother Ransom. The boys, Wilf, Willie, and John Lambdin, were adults and living in Arkansas, Michigan, and Illinois, respectively, but they all rushed to Kansas to do what they could for their aunt.

John Lambdin tells the story of visiting the farmhouse in the company of Sheriff Lessman. While standing in the kitchen having a conversation with the sheriff, John found himself fingering the loose edge of the linoleum countertop. With little effort, he pulled back the linoleum to find it had been lined with $20 bills. Later, when removing the dishes from the cabinet, they discovered that layers of $20 bills had been placed neatly between each plate, saucer, and bowl.

On another occasion, John recalls walking through the chicken coop. A man of more than six feet, he noticed a dusty baking soda tin sitting on a rafter. Thinking that it was an odd place for a can of baking soda, John retrieved the can only to discover a roll of $20 bills tucked inside.

Others reported finding similar stashes of money hidden in odd places around the property and buried in glass pickle jars along the fence row and in flower beds. In how many other places was money hidden and how much had the thieves discovered while ransacking her home?

Amanda Lambdin Dowthitt died on December 10, 1954, in the Viets Nursing Home and was buried beside her father, Wilford Lambdin, in the Mount Hope Cemetery.

No one was ever arrested for this cowardly, greedy act that contributed to Amanda's death. The family and locals had their suspicions, but nothing could be done about it. For years after her death, Amanda's property was ransacked by people searching for her hidden fortune.

Time passed and the specifics of the crime disappeared into local lore. It became a rite of passage of sorts for area teenagers to visit the farm in the dark of night with shovels and dig holes in hopes of finding buried treasure.

Eventually the Independence Municipal Airport and a Cessna manufacturing plant were built in the area, covering with concrete much of what had been Amanda's farm.

For the three years following her death, the attorneys and the probate court deliberated the disbursement of Amanda's estate, which in the end was valued at about $65,000, or nearly a half million dollars in today's money.

Who knows how much the attorneys and courts received for their services? And how much was stolen by the original thieves or found by curious trespassers? And how much remains buried on the Kansas prairie?

Amanda Dowthitt had not had the foresight to create a will and somehow twenty-three people ended up getting a slice of that half-million-dollar pie.

But her nephews, Wilf, Willie, and John, were the largest beneficiaries. John Lambdin was living in Union County, Illinois, at this time and making payments on a 240-acre farm near the town of Wolf Lake in the Mississippi River valley.

One day in 1957, he went to his mailbox and there was the final check from his Aunt Amanda's estate. It was just $8,000 in 1957, but that's more than $60,000 today. He didn't even go in the house or tell his wife, but instead walked directly to his pickup truck and drove to the First National Bank of Grand Tower, where he paid off his farm, free and clear.

John Lambdin was my grandfather, who along with his son Charles, my father, farmed the land until the early 1990s.

According to the will that John Lambdin so thoughtfully prepared, perhaps in part because of the dispute over his Aunt
Amanda's estate, the estate settled quickly and without dispute.
My brother, Randy Lambdin, was given first opportunity to
purchase the farm, which he did without hesitation.

Today the fourth generation of Lambdin farmers work
the land that, in large part, came into our family upon Aunt
Amanda's unfortunate death. It's a place of frequent family cel-
ebrations and community gatherings. We have a cousin Amanda
who was named for our legendary aunt, and she embraces the
family history and legacy to its fullest.

None of us who enjoy the comfort of our family farm today
ever had the opportunity to know Amanda. But we talk of her
often with a mixture of pride and remorse, never forgetting that
out there somewhere in 1954, someone got away with murder.

BIBLIOGRAPHY

Beals, Carleton. *Cyclone Carry.* Philadelphia: Chilton Company, 1962.

Bolig, Jeff, and Doug Vance. *Beware of the Phog: 50 Years of Allen Fieldhouse.* Champaign, IL: Sports Publishing, 2004.

Butler, Susan. *East to the Dawn: The Life of Amelia Earhart.* Reading, MA: Addison-Wesley, 1997.

Carter, Robert A. *Buffalo Bill Cody: The Man Behind the Legend.* Hoboken, NJ: John Wiley Publishing, 2000.

Davis, Kenneth S. *Dwight D. Eisenhower: Soldier of Democracy.* New York: Smithmark Publishers, 1995.

De la Garza, Phyllis. *Death for Dinner.* Honolulu: Talei Publishing, 2004.

Eisenhower, Dwight D. *At Ease: Stores I Tell to Friends.* New York: Doubleday & Company, 1967.

———. *Ike's Letters to a Friend.* Lawrence: University Press of Kansas, 1984.

Grace, Fran. *Carry A. Nation: Retelling the Life.* Bloomington: Indiana University Press, 2004.

Hutton, Paul, and Bill Kurtis. *Investigating History: Dalton Gang Raid.* History Channel Series: Season 1, Episode 11, 2004.

Jameson, W. C. *Buried Treasures of the Great Plains.* Little Rock, AR: August House, 1998.

Johnson, Randy. *A Dispatch to Custer: The Tragedy of Lieutenant Kidder.* Missoula, MT: Mountain Press Publishing, 1999.

Journeys of Hope: Orphan Train Riders, Their Own Stories. Springdale, AR: Orphan Train Heritage Society of America, 1999.

Link, Theodore. *George Armstrong Custer: General of the U.S. Cavalry.* New York: Rosen Publishing Group, 2004.

Morrissey, Muriel Earhart. *Amelia, My Courageous Sister.* Santa Clara, CA: Osborne Publisher, 1987.

Painter, Nell Irvin. *Exodusters: Black Migration to Kansas After Reconstruction.* New York: W. W. Norton, 1976.

Personal correspondence with John Eisenhower, February 2011.

Personal interview with Angela Bates, Nicodemus historian, February 2011.

Personal interview with Grady Atwater, curator, John Brown Memorial Park and Museum, February 2011.

Personal interview with John Alvey, Dalton Defenders Museum, October 2010.

Personal interview with Louise Foudray, caretaker, Amelia Earhart Birthplace Museum, September 2010.

Reis, Ronald A. *Buffalo Bill Cody.* New York: Chelsea House, 2010.

Reynolds, David S. *John Brown, Abolitionist: The Man Who Killed Slavery, Sparked the Civil War, and Seeded Civil Rights.* New York: Alfred A. Knopf, 2005.

Villard, Oswald Garrison. *John Brown, 1800–1859: A Biography Fifty Years After.* Boston: Houghton Mifflin Company, 1910.

Warren, Louis S. *Buffalo Bill's America.* New York: Alfred A. Knopf, 2005.

Wood, Fern Morrow. *The Benders, Keepers of the Devil's Inn.* Cherryvale, KS: F. M. Wood, 1992.

INDEX

ABOUT THE AUTHOR

Diana Lambdin Meyer is a Kansas City–based freelance travel writer. Her lifelong fascination with history and the odd details of life have inspired her to write about the mysteries, myths, and legends that have taken place in Kansas in the past 150 years.

Diana's career as a travel writer has taken her, a farm girl from rural southern Illinois, to some of the farthest reaches of the planet—but some of her favorites stories and journeys have been just down the road and around the corner.

Diana is also the author of *Day Trips from Kansas City* and *Nebraska: Off The Beaten Path* (both Globe Pequot Press). She and her husband/photographer, Bruce, are active members of the Society of American Travel Writers. Follow their journeys at www.mojotraveler.com.